The Federation of Dining Room Professionals (FDRP)®

1417 Sadler Road #100
Fernandina Beach, Amelia Island, Florida 32034
USA

www.FDRP.com
www.FrontSUMMIT.com

904-491-6690

info@FDRP.com

Photographs by:
Mrs. Lorna Smith
The Culinary Institute of America
Federation of Dining Room Professional,LLC
Bitter Root Brewing, Hamilton, MT

Although the models photographed in this book wear uniforms often associated with the performance of service in a dining room of high standing, the techniques and principles exemplified apply to all full-service establishments--regardless of standing or style.

"There is a misconception that service is 'simple', but service is simple only when it is at its finest."

Cindy Martinage, Director, FDRP

V-11

 EXPRESS *Your Hospitality*®

Certified Hospitality Grand Master™

Certified Dining Room Master™

Certified Dining Room Professional™
Certified Steakhouse Professional™

Certified Dining Room Associate™
Certified Associate Wine Steward™

Certified Dining Room Apprentice™

Life Membership

Federation of Dining Room Professionals (FDRP)
1417 Sadler Road # 100
Fernandina Beach, Amelia Island, Florida 32034 - USA
tel 904-491/6690 - fax 904-491/6689 - www.FDRP.com - www.FrontSUMMIT.com

Table of Contents

Table of Contents

Table of Contents

Federation of Dining Room Professionals (FDRP)
1417 Sadler Road # 100
Fernandina Beach, Amelia Island, Florida 32034 - USA
tel 904-491/6690 - fax 904-491/6689
www.FDRP.com - www.FrontSUMMIT.com

The standards of performance for the techniques of service presented in this program are based on the *International Business & Gourmet Standards of Hospitality* (IBGS of Hospitality).

The Beverage Service Standards portion of this course, which is also included in the IBGS Standards, has received *The International Sommelier Guild* (ISG) Seal of Approval

This program is endorsed by and is the recipient of the *American Culinary Federation* (ACF) *Educational Assurance Award* since 2005.

1 | Introduction

This introduction provides:

- Insights from the FDRP Founder.

- Ladder to Success
  (Overview of Certification Levels).

- Valuable information on the
  organization of these manuals.

- Acknowledgements.

- William Rice on Service Evolution.

SECTION ONE

Introduction

Overview

This section reviews . . .

- Insights from the Founder.

- FDRP Certification levels and prerequisites.

- Organization of The Guide series.

- Acknowledgements.

- William Rice on Service Evolution.

Introduction

From the Founder

Conglomerates, companies, and individuals are all entities that must make decisions and take actions on a daily basis. And whether big or small these decisions impact the organization and its surroundings in many ways. Often the foundation of decisions is more important that the actual decision, and even though there is a clear right and wrong way of doing most things, there are still grey areas - especially in defining a key element of decision making: priorities. That is because priorities change depending on where one is located in the organization. The priorities that preoccupy a floor person differ from a manager's priorities, which differ from executive levels, and so forth. Priorities also change laterally: A chef has different priorities than a waiter, and so on. But we all have a responsibility and a priority to be professional.

When asked to define Professionalism in Service, my answer is that professionalism in the hospitality industry is the combination of these three elements into the execution of each task, with the outcome being revenue:

- Knowledge
- Skills
- Attitude

The content of FDRP's work and all the programs within FDRP are entirely based

FDRP Founder, Bernard Martinage

on the skills, knowledge, attitude and the tools with which I established my successes in the hospitality industry.

From a personal point of view, professionalism represents my dedication to do the right things for the right reasons. It is my ability to balance the different priorities that are asked of me, in the execution of my duties, while maintaining the highest level of harmony with my associates.

For example, when managing the restaurant Escoffier at The Culinary Institute of America in Hyde Park, New York, at the time the flagship restaurant of the Institute, my priorities were many, various, and often contradictory. If you are reading this book you know exactly the feeling I am expressing here. I had customers driving up to two hours from Manhattan with expectations in line with their travel time. To serve them I had a staff made of culinary students, who were less than two months from graduation and whose enthusiasm for studying at all -- but especially for the front-of-the-house training -- was understandably low. And, of course, I had two bosses: Director of Restaurant Operations and Certified Master Chef, Tom Peer, who had expectations of revenue and business performance from the restaurant; and, Associate Dean, Ezra Eichelberger, who's priorities lie with how his primary clients-the students-are being managed. From both gentlemen I learned a lot and found inspiration that is a big part of FDRP today.

One may think that there is no way to meet opposing objectives without detriment to one or the other. Yet, in the three years I spent at the CIA the following happened:

- Escoffier became the first student-staffed restaurant in the US to earn a five-star rating.
- Escoffier became the first-and is still the only-student-staffed restaurant to enter the Nation's Restaurant News Fine Dining Hall of Fame.
- I was elected three times by my students to be their faculty speaker at Commencement.
- The restaurant made more revenue than ever before.
- The restaurant was featured on live, National television throughout its specialty dining event series that people still discuss today.

Even after leaving the Institute over ten years ago, I am pleased to still be connected to many of my former students. Everybody won. The reason for me to explain all of this in this introduction is to show you that it is possible to do it all when you have your priorities properly aligned and use the right tools. The tools I used to build my career, the FDRP, and this book are as follows:

Integrity

In our industry we touch people's lives in many many ways. By the simple fact that we serve them nourishment for their body and provide everyone the same hospitality regardless of their wealth, fame, or other differences, we create a place where our customers can be comfortable and enjoy a great meal. For the modest income couple treating themselves out to dinner at the finest restaurant should be made to feel as special as the movie star that visits the same establishment. I believe it is an honor for professional hosts to be able to deliver special memories to people.

William Arnot put it best:

"If honor be your clothing, the suit will last a lifetime; but if clothing be your honor, it will soon be worn threadbare."

Being a person of integrity also involves more than having honor. It also includes being a 'get it done' type of individual. How many people can you name who when they promise something you know that you can count on it being done . . . really?

Keeping your integrity is difficult because, sadly, the more integrity you have the more pressure you will feel to abandon it. "Peer pressure" can create an antagonistic atmosphere where the push to change will be strong. You will end up asking yourself if you should loosen your integrity to ease your life, or be ready to defend it for what you know is right. Many times in my career I was visited by colleagues who sometimes went as far as threatening me in an attempt to convince me to stop doing so well because they didn't want to have to do the same. My answer to them comes from Winston Churchill: *"Never give up."*

Determination
Determination in this context also includes Focus. If your will fades as the day, the week or the month grows long, then you pretty much are starting at square one every day, week or month. Continuity and focus are essential to accomplish anything of meaningful size that will last, have an impact on people, and possess the ability for others to bene-fit.

Simplicity
Keep things simple. It is easy to get wrapped up in the politics or details of an event or an operation. Remind yourself of what it is that you are trying to achieve,

what and who you have as an asset to accomplish it, and make the safest plan to success you can conceive. Make sure that your base structure is solid and that you do not commit these two mistakes: 1) Doing something for yourself rather than the benefit of the organization, and 2) Being isolated in decisions rather than using a trusted team.

Kindness
Success, and I mean long term success, depends on good hospitality. So if you are a serious and mindful host, you must be in it for the good of others and simply deal with the tough moments. Never be stingy with your knowledge. Yes, knowledge is power, but if you think that it is what you know and others don't that sets you apart then you are doomed to fail. I spent my career sharing what I knew and even gave classes to colleagues at my home over weekends to improve the team. By being giving and kind you earn trust, confi-dence, dedication and loyalty--none of which that can genuinely purchased and all of which are of what the greatest success stories are made. Your learn more by teaching than by anything else.

Recognize the people who helped you and what you learned from them! I founded the FDRP using all the principles I am describing to you. The content FDRP offers today is the sum of all the knowl-edge gained from every interaction I had over my lifetime. There are too numerous people to acknowledge here, but you can find several listed in this book.

That said, regardless of the quality of the content you are acquiring today, it is the use that YOU will make of it and the decisions that YOU will make that will determine how people will respond to you and where your career will take you.

A professional person with the qualities I describe in this introduction has all the tools to become a cornerstone, not only to an establishment, but also to a company of any size, plus his/her community and society as a whole. The quality you strive to achieve determines almost instantly the opportunities that will be presented to you, at ev-er-y level of your life.

Your involvement in this certification program shows that you are already taking your career and goals-be they what they may-a step further than many other professionals. Certification is in many ways a unique form of recognition. It cannot be earned through study alone; it cannot be earned by experience alone; it requires knowledge, skills, attitude, and symbolizes dedication, accomplishment, and peer recognition.

Once you achieve certification you become an integral part of the hospitality industry, albeit a cornerstone in the pyramid of success that makes the industry and certification attractive to others. You become a source of inspiration, respect and trust. You are shaping the hospitality industry. Whether serving is perceived as an honorable and worthy career path or is seen as an interim profession is entirely based on the way you represent it and the inspiration you provide others.

Blessings

The hospitality industry is the second largest employer in the United States. During your career you will be addressing generations of employees at different stages of their own career. You will also be serving generations of customers at different stages of their lives. These volumes of The Professional Service Guide as well as its worthy certification will provide you with the technical and business aspects of our industry, but you still need to provide the inspiration and integrity.

Your service of excellence to the industry and the people you serve will make memories that will stay with your customers for the rest of their lives. You will witness engagements, family reunions, dates, and many other moments in your customer's life for which they will have chosen to trust you. Some of these memories will become yours as well; your life will become richer for it and your perspective of humanity will be changed forever.

This is the profession you chose, and it will be incredible if you let it.

Ladder to Success

Being acknowledged as one of the most essential components of customer satisfaction and restaurant success improves staff moral while increasing sales.

Stand Out
Whether it is by your staff or manager, being recognized as having certification credentials is a distinction worthy of respect. It says you have not only proven that you have technical skillfulness, but have also mastered the hospitality expertise of a true professional.

What FDRP certification means to your staff or students:
- Recognition translates into happier staff, which tends to stay where they are appreciated
- Reward learning by pairing certification with either an increase in pay or a promotion
- Certification designation differentiates you from others applying for the same job opportunity
- Validation of a career choice and hospitality experience

What FDRP certification means about an employer or educational institute:
- You value and validate the skills of current staff or job applicants
- Your training program is part of a National, award-winning standard

- You recognize that dining room skills and safety standards are for all restaurants, regardless of their style or standing
- You promote professional development and career growth for staff

Certification Programs
From Apprentice and Associate, to the progressive Professional and Master levels, each program is designed to build practiced service professionals with a strong understanding of the techniques, knowledge and management experience that can be applied to any style of restaurant -- regardless of its cuisine or complexity of service.

———— PROGRAM COMPARISON OVERVIEW ————

This career path recognizes the wealth of knowledge that hospitality professionals possess and allows recognition of their experience through the passing of each level.

Apprentice Program

- No alcohol module
- Designed for underage culinarians
- High school curriculum
  - Teacher Kit
  - Student Manual

Certified Dining Room Apprentice™

Associate Program

- Alcohol and Service modules
- Self study or instructor led
- Designed for integration into
  - Culinary Institutions
  - Hospitality Organizations
- Spanish option

Certified Dining Room Associate™
Certified Associate Wine Steward™

Professional Program

- Translate experience into credentials
- Designed to enhance
  - Staff transition across units
  - Employee retention
- Build management skills

Certified Dining Room Professional™
Certified Steakhouse Professional™

Master Program

- Ultimate career credential
- Designed to include lodging professionals
- Distinction for hospitality achievements

Certified Hospitality Grand Master™

Certified Dining Room Master™

Organization of Manuals

The Professional Service Guide is printed as a series of four independent volumes. Created so that one can quickly find a desired topic within a given subject matter, The Guide is divided into the following knowledge areas:

1) Operations Management
2) Culinary Essentials
3) Service Essentials
4) Tableside Secrets and
   Advanced Techniques

Since each volume and each section within a volume is self-contained, the reader can go directly to any session for thorough knowledge on topics ranging from cost control to wine.

Operations Management
This volume provides a high-level overview of critical elements of management knowledge. While by no means an all-inclusive book on management skills, this volume is geared to provide managers and especially those new to the management role, general explanations on labor, ethics, training, and customer interactions. The aspects of the internal and external environments that influence how management and employees perform their duties are introduced alongside key elements of restaurant organization.

Culinary Essentials
This volume focuses on the mass of culinary knowledge that professional servers should have to perform at their peak. Covering items from cuisine styles and cooking methods to details on cuts and categories of vegetable, seafood, meats, and poultry, this comprehensive reference guide even delves into cocktails, beer, wine and tableside decanting.

Service Essentials
This volume contains a wealth of information on the basic techniques and skills all front-of-the-house professionals need. The most popular set up styles are reviewed plus an overview on service of coffee and other beverages, plus wine. A wide variety of topics are detailed in this general practices and table maintenance guide.

Tableside Secrets and Advanced Techniques
This volume contains both important information on safety, knife handling skills, and numerous tableside step-by-step recipes.

With Thanks

The FDRP would like to acknowledge several individuals, faculty members and schools who contributed to the certification process and the creation of this reference guide. Their evaluations, suggestions and contributions have enhanced the quality of this body of work.

Cindy Martinage for her editing and formatting skills, plus other varied contributions to the overall project.

Frederic B. Mayo, Ph.D. C.H.E., for his contribution of the Introduction to Teaching chapter included in this introduction and his excellent editing suggestions.

Gil Kulers, for his contribution of the entire Wine Essentials section.

John Feiler for his wonderful contributions on Kitchen Controversial.

Denis Commergnat for the excellent write-up on Caviar.

Chef Brandon Walker for his wonderful Fish review.

David A. Swanson, DRM, for his contribution of the entire Beer Essentials section, several chapters in the Cooking Essentials section, plus his consistent availability for many photo shoots.

Chef Victor Mathews for his detailed work on Beef and involvement in the certification process.

Ming Chu Lin (Pearl), Matt Moore, and Kevin Shireman, for their consistent availability for many photo shoots that seemed to always last way into the night.

Alicia Pokoik, for her discussion on Restrictive Diets.

Chef Lon Symensma, for providing all the definitions found in Cooking Essentials.

Foodservice Profitability, A Control Approach, Second Edition (Prentice Hall, 2001) by Edward E. Sanders and Timothy H. Hill, referenced several times in Operations Management volume and for the entire chapter: Control Practices Applied to Human Resources Issues, Gratuities, Wage Laws, and Working Conditions.

The Culinary Institute of America (CIA), for granting to the FDRP the right to use their facilities, equipment, and for providing most of the pictures documenting the Cooking Essentials. See detail listing located in the rear of this manual.

William Rice on Service Evolution

William Rice, Food and Wine Columnist for the Chicago Tribune.

Two major things distinguish service today from what it was say, 20 to 50 years ago," Rice begins. "First, it has become quite improvisational, as wait persons have to interact with their guests in a way they never had to in the past. Every customer, table or group is going to be different so servers need to be amateur psychologists. Second, it is becoming more of a require-ment to have an in-depth knowledge of things that used to be relegated to the chef or sommelier, such as dishes, sauces and wines."

These two qualities compliment one another and, together, are helping to change service in America. A look at the history of dining out in this country in the last half-century, much of it witnessed first-hand by Rice, shows how this evolu-tion occurred.each program is designed to build practiced service professionals with a strong understanding of the techniques, knowledge and management experience that can be applied to any style of restau-rant -- regardless of its cuisine or complex-ity of service.

At the turn of the 20th century, ordinary people didn't eat out. When George Gibbs took Emily Webb to get a strawberry phosphate in Thornton Wilder's Our Town, it was a really big deal. Mr. Morgan, the druggist, made it even more special by serving them with flourish and stating, "Here they are. Enjoy 'em." For the most part, women were the chefs and servers of the day. To go outside the home for a good meal was rare. Boarding houses and inns began in small numbers before and during World War I, but the norm was still the in-home, family-style service. By the 1920s, some family-owned roadside dining rooms had emerged in rural areas as travel by automobile expanded.

During the 1930s and into the '40s some elegant restaurants opened in the major cities, but Prohibition, the Great Depression and World War II, kept dining out an activ-ity accessible only to well-to-do Americans.

Dining out was not at all as spontaneous as

it is today. It was either a special occasion or event, like an anniversary, or a planned night once a month. "People were more family oriented. They'd go to grandma's house for Sunday dinner, not a restaurant."

The 1940s did see the beginning of more democratized service, even though dining out was not yet a standard way of life. "In those days it was an excuse to get together and drink," Rice says. "The food was secondary. If a customer ordered a steak the only questions would be, 'Is it big? Is it juicy?' That was the only level of food expectation."

Those few questions, however, were the basis for the types of interactions between the wait staff and customers we see today. Rice also points out that very few people drank wine, and that just the emergence of wine service made a huge impact on what waiters of today are expected to do. But 60 years ago, there were fewer restaurant levels from which to dine and, therefore, fewer levels of service.

Typically, diners chose from either the comfortable, very relaxed style of restaurant or the staunch, European (mostly French) service style. These two dining experiences are at opposite ends of the dining spectrum. Rice notes, "In the French model, everyone had a role and played it. Chefs had a ritual, classically trained waiters had a ritual and there was very little improvisation. Frankly, it was a lot easier to be a waiter in those days because everyone knew what to do."

In general, the knowledge that a waiter needed to successfully perform his job was smaller in scope, too. A waiter didn't have to learn the menu because often it was the same, day in and day out, year after year. That meant a waiter could walk through his job with certain skills but didn't have to interact with the customer or the kitchen to any great extent. "Of course there were some innovative chefs in those days, but essentially customer expectations were within a certain parameter."

The 1950s and early '60s brought a broadening of eateries with the return of soldiers who went into the workplace and chose to live in something new--the suburbs. Drive-in restaurants sprang up, as cars were no longer just a luxury.

"There wasn't fast food yet, but there were coffee shops, luncheonettes and delis and customers took service for granted. It was a basic style of service, but you couldn't stay in business without it. Servers began to interact a little more with customers, but they still didn't interface much with the cooks about the dishes and their ingredients."

The 1970s ushered in a multitude of "theme" restaurants and the '80s saw a proliferation of international and ethnic establishments heretofore isolated in certain communities. Chain restaurants at both ends of the dining spectrum appeared at the same time and by the end of the century, most Americans were eating out at least once a week. But even today, Americans are still somewhat intimidated by the European style of service.

It can be perceived as condescending, someone simply going through the motions instead of the warm interchange that's desired. Part of the changing standards is that diners want a waiter who is a participant in the meal, not someone who hands them a sheet, writes things down, brings the food back and puts it down. They want to ask about things and want intelligent answers. Rice elaborates. "In Europe, a diner looks up and sees a uniform. In America he looks up and sees a person." The European style can be more regimented because it's not as personal. A waiter notices that the cheese knife is missing and fetches the cheese knife.

Americans, in general, are more democratic in their thinking and are not comfortable with the concept of servants, Rice believes. So an American waiter might say, "You seem to be missing a cheese knife. Let me get you one." It's a more comfortable scenario for Americans.

William Rice thinks that today's opportunities in service are due to the new American lifestyle in which people like to go out and expect a gratifying experience, not just food.

As a result he finds that there has been a steady improvement in almost every aspect of the restaurant business--from cooks and servers to rituals and processes--which he sees continuing into the future.

"There is no question in my mind that we are working our way to an American style of service which is neither as militaristic and strict as original European service nor as off-hand and casual as the 'Hi-My-Name's Bruce' style of the '60s and '70s."

Filling this service need, he believes there are a coterie of young people who take this work seriously and find themselves challenged by all the knowledge they are required to have and are attracted by the good income, better opportunities and customers who want their input. "We already see more and more culinarian graduates taking positions in the dining room. That means that in the near future instead of 'I'm an actor, but I'm currently waiting tables,' you'll soon hear, 'I have a hospitality degree from Named school,' or 'I am a certified professional.'"

It's not surprising that media coverage of the hospitality industry increased as the volume of dining out did. As the food dollar spent away from home continues to increase from 25% in 1955 to 46% in 2001 to a projected 53% by 2010, Americans in the future will look even more to the media for ratings of food, value and service experience.

Here is a timeline of some of the more notable events:

Before 1940
- Media coverage was very limited. There were a handful of papers with food editors but not a lot of people who knew about them or cared.

1940s
- Gourmet magazine debuted in 1941 and was the only periodical dedicated to food.
- Duncan Hines, a seasoned traveler, wrote about his experiences, most notably in a book called Adventures in Good Eating.
- Press coverage began to increase as WWII veterans had created some interest in Asian and Europeans cuisines.
- The Culinary Institute of America opens in 1946.

1950s
- Lucius Beebe writes columns about food and wine.
- Mr. Holiday, a traveling salesman starts the Holiday magazine, which became Travel and Holiday, covered food and restaurants regularly and started national restaurant awards, the only national awards at that time.

1970s
- William Rice and Burton Wolf land "Where To Eat in America", a national restaurant guide.
- Tim and Nina Zagat start what will become the nationally acclaimed gourmet resource and review: ZagatSurvey®.

1980s
- The James Beard Foundation is created in honor of Mr. James Beard, recognized as the father of American gastronomy.

1990s
- Saveur magazine is launched along with a new wave of food and nutrition publications.
- FDRP becomes the first hospitality certification body to offer certification credentials ranging from Apprentice to Master and to publish a magazine 100% dedicated to service: Pro-Success.

Today
- Columnists like William Rice are faithfully read in a multitude of newspapers and journals.
- Food Channels, broadcast food shows 24/7.
- Food related publications have multiplied by 10 times in the last 20 years.
- Culinary schools has multiplied by 10 times in the last 30 years.
- The hospitality industry is the second largest employer in America after the government.
- Johnson & Wales University and Kendall College, become the first major institutions to require service certification in their culinary programs.
- FDRP becomes the first organization to earn the endorsement of the American Culinary Federation (ACF), the International Sommelier Guild (ISG) and to negotiate successfully governmental reciprocity with the Canadian Government.

2 | Cooking Essentials

This section you will learn how to:

- Cooking Essentials
    - Cuisine Styles
    - Cuisine Flairs
    - Cooking Methods
    - Cooking Temperatures
    - Vegetable Cuts
    - Seafood
    - Meats
    - Poultry and Game Birds
    - Stocks, Soups & Sauces
    - Garde Manger
    - Baking and Pastry Terms
    - Restrictive Diets
    - Allergies

SECTION TWO

Cooking Essentials

Overview

By the end of this section, you should be able to...

- Differentiate between cuisine styles.

- Differentiate the most commonly used flairs by country of origin.

- Understand the different moist and dry heat cooking methods.

- Differentiate different vegetable cuts.

- List fish categories and give examples of each.

- List meat categories and give examples of each.

- State the difference between poultry and game birds.

- Identify Mother Sauces and Contemporary Sauces.

- Identify thickeners and commonly used soups.

- Differentiate between common restrictive diets.

- List examples of food items to avoid for specific food allergies.

Cooking Essentials

A dining room professional is an ambassador for the kitchen. Beyond the responsibility to provide genuine hospitality and a consistent level of service, the dining room professional benefits from developing a comprehensive understanding of food. A professional server is a partner to the Chef by providing guests with the best match to their dining expectations. This is only possible after servers establish a good line of communication with the kitchen staff. One way to earn the respect of chefs is to demonstrate a knowledge and appreciation for the art of food preparation, which chefs have dedicated their lives.

Cuisine Styles

HAUTE CUISINE

From the French word, meaning 'high', this classical European style of cooking, which is typically French, is mostly accessible to members of high society and nobility, due to its high cost.

Haute cuisine is characterised by elaborate preparations and presentations served in small and numerous courses that were produced by large and hierarchical staffs at the grand restaurants and hotels of Europe.

NOUVELLE CUISINE

Figure 1: New Bouilabaisse

This cuisine was the first to migrate away from the heavy, rich style of classical French cuisine by incorporating the use of fresher, lighter ingredients.

This style uses the principles of natural reduction instead of heavy thickeners.

Food has to be presented in an artistic manner playing with colors and forms, and the plate has to be arranged as a work of art similar to a sculpture or a painting.

FUSION CUISINE

The style of cooking that marries ingredients and techniques of different geographical areas together. Wolfgang Puck is considered as one of the pioneers of fusion cuisine. An example this type of course would be a Korean Taco.

MOLECULAR COOKING

In an increasing effort to push the culinary envelope, chefs from around the world are turning to the use of chemicals in their kitchens to create new textures and presentations on their plates. These chemicals along with cutting edge techniques have turned some restaurants into what would appear to be a chemistry lab with a dining room attached. At Restaurant Moto in Chicago for example, all the chefs are themselves waiters--both creating the dishes in their kitchen and then serving them to their guests. This combo-role allows them to directly field the many questions that are inevitably aroused by their shocking creations.

Sodium Alginate & Calcium Chloride: Spheres, Caviar & Ravioli

Sodium Alginate and Calcium Chloride are used in conjunction to create flavorful, sphere-shaped 'ravioli' that has an interesting caviar-like quality. The Sodium Alginate is incorporated into a base of water which is flavored using the ingredient of choice, such as tea, black olive, basil, squid ink or tomato; the flavoring possibilities are virtually endless.

The "alginate" is an algae-based thickener (think lemon meringue pie filling) and quickly firms up this mixture to resemble loose Jell-O. Meanwhile a water bath containing the Calcium Chloride (a salt used in cheese production) is prepared.

The flavored alginate mixture is dropped into the water bath using a small measuring spoon or syringe to create the desired shape and size of the finished sphere. A reaction between the alginate and the calcium chloride encapsulates the flavor in a thin, gelatinous shell which thickens the longer the item remains in the bath.

Figure 2: Melon Ball using Sodium Alginate & Calcium Chloride

Once a desired thickness is achieved these delicate spheres are removed, rinsed and reserved for the presentation. The end result is much like a poached egg yolk that remains runny in the center while holding is shape covered in a thin cooked layer.

Tapioca Maltodextrin: Powders, Dusts & Sand

As the name suggests, this ingredient is derived from tapioca, a starch extracted from the root of the Cassava plant, commonly used as a thickening agent. Also referred to by its trade name, "N-Zorbit", Tapioca Maltodextrin is a lighter-than-air powder that has a remarkable ability to absorbed moisture but its principle kitchen application is to create flavorful, literally mouth watering powders from liquefied fats such as olive oil, bacon and even chocolate.

Tapioca Maltodextrin is carefully incorporated into the fat at a high 2:1 ratio creating a sandy, lightly-colored mixture. This mixture can be further refined by sifting to intensify its color and mouth feel.

The resulting application can be used as a curiously flavorful garnish or even as a substitute for other components, such as the anchovy for a Caesar salad.

Transglutaminases: Meat Glue

Transglutaminases is a finely granulated, tasteless powder that has been used in the meat processing industry since the mid 1950's and has found its way into today's trendy kitchens.

As a protein binder, its use is to create more esthetically pleasing presentations

Figure 3: Tuna Duo - ahi & escolar terrine created using Transglutaminases

Photo courtesy of Chef Richard Gras, Salt, The Grill, Ritz Carlton, Amelia Island, FL.

such as a roulade of meat that doesn't fall apart once it has been cooked and sliced. The binding properties of this ingredient help to maintain a seamless and cohesive product that holds its shape without impacting the item's overall flavor or texture.

Transglutaminases is made up of a family of enzymes that act as protein binders for a variety of culinary applications. It can be used to seamlessly bind different fish together, such as tuna and salmon, creating a dual-textured and two-toned effect.

With meat dishes, bacon will adhere to the outside of a filet or a steak can easily be sutured back in place following the removal of the center eye of fat.

Lecithin: Foam, Air & Froth

"Foams" are the quintessential elements of the modern kitchen that have been widely used to add a lightly flavored and textured element to a dish. Much like the froth that tops a well-made cappuccino, this creation is one of the very first to be used by cutting-edge chefs to express flavors and sensations in a stunningly new way.

Somewhat over-used in today's kitchens, it is the challenge of the chef to create a froth that not only has flavor, but complements (while not distracting from) the other components of the dish. A foam or froth can be created using intensely flavored and colored items such as beets, carrots and basil. Incorporating air into these ingredients is the trick that helps to soften their intense flavors and colors, while adding volume and height to a plate's presentation.

So, what does this have to do with Lecithin? Lecithin is an ingredient (you guessed it, a powder) that is derived from soybeans and is extracted while processing its oils. Lecithin functions as an emulsifier (incorporate or bind two elements that would normally not mix with one another such as oil and water) and helps to stabilize foams and froths. Lecithin is added to a flavorful liquid such as carrot juice or wasabi powder dissolved in water, and aerated using an emersion blender to 'beat up' the top of the liquid. From there the

Figure 4: Carrot Froth (Lecithin stabilized Carrot Juice) over white beans & Boudin Noir.

Photo courtesy of Chef Richard Gras, Salt, The Grill, Ritz Carlton, Amelia Island, FL.

foam is scooped off the top of the liquid and spooned onto the dish. This mixture may also be used in a whipped cream charger or canister to create a densely textured froth with the benefit of added stability.

From a server's stand point it is helpful to understand how the molecular influence is used in a dish and communicate the chef's intention more effectively with your guests. The textures and presentations created by chef chemists in the kitchen will spark conversation and arouse interest in your guests. By being prepared to discuss these and other culinary trends with customers, a server gains credibility and will enrich their dining experience!

Cuisine Flair, per County of Origin

―――――――――――― ITALIAN ――――――――――――

The Italian people believe that cooking is based upon preserving the characteristic tastes of separate ingredients, more than by blending flavors together. Their approach is very direct and natural. Little attention is paid to complex sauces and timely preparations. Cooking depends enormously on the quality of the ingredients found locally. Italy is divided into twenty (20) regions, each with its own culinary identity.

Figure 5: Italy

Piedmont

Figure 6: Proscuitto

The cuisine of Italy's Piedmont region is hearty and full of powerful flavors. Wild game meats and foraged mushrooms are common.

Black truffles are harvested here and rice is a staple over pasta or polenta. Garlic and strong cheeses are also prevalent. Prosciutto, a salt cured and dry aged pork, is made from the more tender and lean cuts of the pork, such as the loin.

Wines from this region are predominately made from either Mebbiolo or Barbara grapes. Powerful Barolo and Barbaresco wines are the hallmark of the region.

Veneto

Risotto is Veneto's most well-known dish and is indicative of the rich, full flavored dishes found in this region. Spices and heavy sauces are common. Marinated anchovies and seafood become more popular towards the Adriatic coast; sausages and game meats are found inland.

Bitter greens and radicchio as well as asparagus are popular here. A typical dish of the region consists of sautéed liver and onions.

Wines from this region include Amarone, which is well known for it's dried fruit aroma. Prosecco, one of Italy's sparkling wines, is produced here.

Figure 7: Sausage

Emilia-Romagna

Emilia-Romagna's Bologna is well known for its egg based pastas. Rich and hearty tomato sauces with meat are common whereas rice is less popular. Polenta made from corn meal is a staple starch.

Balsalmic vinegar from Modena is known the world over as are the Parma hams and Mortadella sausages.

Figure 8: Tomato sauce and pasta

Tuscany

Figure 9: White Truffles

Tuscany is in the heart of Italy and it's cuisine hinges on simplicity. A wide variety of ingredients from the legumes and cheeses, to breads and vegetables are staples.

Explosively fragrant White Truffles are found here briefly between October and November.

High quality beef and pork along with olive oils are frequently used in this region's cooking.

Campania

Figure 10: Pizza with mozzerella

Campania's cuisine is much lighter than the regions to the north. Fresh tomatoes, peppers, fennel and lemon are commonly used throughout the region.

Pizza has its origins in this region and many of the more familiar, Italian-American dishes have roots in Campania.

This region is also home of fresh Buffalo Mozzarella, made from the milk of the water buffalo.

GERMAN

German food is famous for being substantial and served in large portions. Meat and potatoes in the form of roasts, sausages and dumplings are the trademarks of this country's cuisine. Sauerkraut, apples and many sweet/savory combinations are also found throughout Germany.

This country is typically divided into three regions:

- The north (cold climate region)
- The central (beer/rye bread/ham)
- The south (lighter cooking)

Figure 11: Germany

North Germany

The north is a cold climate region that is influenced by Scandinavians. The cuisine is filled with thick soups, plus smoked and pickled fishes.

Red fruit and currant puddings as well as rhubarb desserts are also common. These bitter-sweet desserts are often served with vanilla ice cream or heavy cream.

Figure 12: Rhubarb and Cream

Central Germany

Figure 13: German Beer

Central Germany is known for the beer, rye bread, and ham trilogy.

Beer as well as wine from Germany are renowned the world over. Beers come in a wide variety -- from dark and heavy to light and crisp.

Wines, however, are mostly white and Germany's Rieslings are very popular.

South Germany

Figure 14: Apples and cherries

Southern Germany produces lighter cooking based on game and white wine. Potato dumplings and noodles are popular in this area.

Dishes use a sweeter style of mustard than is found in other regions. Schnapps, such as Obstler, which is distilled from apples and pears, and Kirschwasser that is distilled from cherries, are also preferred in the southern region.

RUSSIAN

Figure 15: Russia

Russian cuisine is a basic core of traditional dishes that typify "Old Russia." Cooking is mostly defined by the housewife than from the sumptuous dinner services, embroidered cloths and elaborate parties hosted by the royal families, which were based on French influences.

Hors d'oeuvres served with vodka, smoked fish, caviar, grains, root vegetables and tea are commonly served throughout the country.

Mediterranean style dishes characterize the State of Georgia, while Armenian cookery has an Oriental flavor, and the Ukraine was known as the breadbasket of Europe and has strong German influences.

Central Asia is famous for its fruit, especially melons, while the Baltic States are known for their seafood.

Figure 16: Smoked fish and caviar

Figure 17: Various Melons

LATIN

Figure 18: Fried green chilies

South American food has many influences: by the African slaves, Spanish, Portuguese, Dutch, French, British, Italian, German and the Indian civilizations (Aztec, Maya and Inca).

The cuisine varies greatly from country to country, depending on which groups of people inhabited them. Meat, red beans, rice, potatoes, corn, chilies, tropical fruits, coffee and chocolate are greatly used throughout this region.

Latin cooking is honest and simply prepared. The emphasis is placed on fried foods, open-air grilling and highly spiced dishes.

JAPANESE

Figure 19: Japan

Japanese gastronomy is defined by clarity, lightness, simplicity and order.

The main focus is to serve every product at the right season. Much attention is paid to the setting of the table and the intricate presentation of each dish.

Color, texture and shape are just as important as the flavor of the food. Frying, broiling, marinating, steaming and simmering in a flavorful liquid are the more common cooking techniques.

Soybeans are a main staple, which is used to make miso, soy sauce and tofu.

Rice is widely used in both savory and sweet applications. Served either raw or cooked, seafood plays a major role in Japanese cuisine.

Figure 20: Sashimi with Miso sauce

CHINESE

In China, there is no dividing line between philosophy, religion and food. Chinese meals are full of symbolism and the quest for harmony.

The originality of this cuisine is expressed by mixing four basic flavors: sour, salty, bitter and sweet. Foods are generally cut into small pieces and stir-fried in a wok. Rice, eggs, pancakes and steamed bread rolls are popular.

In the north, food is often simmered in a broth. Soy sauce is the basis for "red cooking" in the east. Western and central China use a lot of dried fish, mushrooms and crystallized fruits, while the south relies on fresh seafood.

Figure 21: Mixing flavors

SPANISH

Figure 22: Paiella

Spanish food is attractively appetizing in the simplest possible way.

It is rarely over-decorated and is more concerned with good ingredients that have been well combined.

Dishes vary from the south with its use of rice and pork, to the north where beef and potatoes are prominent.

The south utilizes lamb and chickpeas while fish and shellfish are caught along the coast and are usually fried.

Small appetizers called tapas are eaten with a glass of wine in local bars and cafes.

UNITED KINGDOM

Cooking of the British Isles is a true testament to "comfort food."

The focus is not on elegant, highly contrived food, but rather on homemade, homegrown products.

The people in the United Kingdon eat a lot of beef and have perfected the art of roasting. Fish & Chips was created in tribute to the plentiful waters.

Figure 23: United Kingdon

A traditional large breakfast is served, and a variety of cheeses are generally offered after a meal.

Sweet or savory puddings are washed down with beer, cider or tea.

Leeks from Wales, turnips from Scotland, cabbage, apples and berries are some common produce from the area.

Figure 24: English Breakfast

FRENCH

At the beginning of the twentieth century, French cooking gained supremacy throughout the world.

A man by the name of Auguste Escoffier developed a system of organization and way of recipe documentation that is still followed by many.

Today, the cuisine of France varies greatly: from butter, cream and foie gras to olive oil, tomatoes and garlic.

Simplicity through perfecting the basic cooking fundamentals is intensified by lavish sauces.

Figure 25: Auguste Escoffier

Paris

Figure 26: Duck

The capital city of Paris is home to more than 9,000 restaurants that represent nearly every cuisine style from Frances' 21 other regions and the world over.

French culture and dining go hand in hand. In Paris one can find a place to eat at every corner from a café on the sidewalk to the world's most renowned restaurants.

Some of the most acclaimed Michelin-rated restaurants can be found in Pairs. The one-star La Tour D'Argent is famous for its Pressed Duck presentation, while the Plaza Athénée houses Alain Ducasse's three-star restaurant.

Champagne & Alsace

Figure 27: Canard Duchene Champagne

The region of Champagne is home to the sparkling wine of the same name. To be labeled 'Champagne' the wine must be produced in this region.

Alsace to the east is heavily influenced by Germany, as is evident in the cuisine.

Choucroute Garnie is a typical Alsatian dish that consists of sauerkraut, sausage, salted pork and potatoes.

Spätzle, a noodle-like dumpling with German origins is also popular here. The Riesling, Pinot Blanc and Gewürztraminer produced here are perfect complements to the local fare.

Normandy & Brittany

The regions of Normandy and Brittany are heavily influenced by the sea. Crustraceans such as langoustine, crawfish and lobsters, as well as fish including monkfish and sole, are indicative of the area.

World-class butter and cheeses are found throughout Normandy.

The cauliflower, artichokes and buckwheat grown here are among the best in France. The buckwheat is used to make thin pancakes or crépes and is a Norman specialty.

Figure 28: French cheeses

Burgundy

Like other regions in France, Burgundy is known for its wines, and although mainly two grapes are grown here, that being Chardonnay and Pinot Noir, the region has a reputation for producing some of the finest wines in the world.

Dishes from Burgundy, such as Boeuf Bourguignon, are rustic and hearty. Ingredients found here range from perch and crabs in the rivers to poultry, smoked meats and game.

Dijon mustard has its home in the northern parts of this region and the black currants grown here are used to make cassis, a sweetened liqueur. Cassis added to still white wine is called a Kir; when added to sparkling wine it is called a Kir Royale.

Figure 29: Black Currants

Bordeaux & Gascony

Figure 30: Sheep

The Bordeaux region has a versatile geography that extends from the Atlantic Ocean to the foothills of the Pyrenees Mountains.

Fishing at the sea and in the streams, as well as trapping small game, are popular. High quality lamb and beef are produced here as are sheep's milk cheeses.

As a wine growning region, Bordeaux produces nearly 800 million bottles of wine annually. Some of the world's top wines are created here.

Provence

Figure 31: Olive Oil and Vegetables

The cuisine of Provence is heavily influenced by the Mediterranean. Provence is also one of France's largest producers of citrus and other fruits, vegetables and herbs.

Naturally, seafood is common along the coast, however dried sausages, lamb and goat's milk cheeses are also found here.

Olives, olive oil and tomatoes are commonly used in Provençal dishes and the honey and lavender grown here is known the world over.

INDIAN

The foods of India are influenced by the various religious practices of the subcontinent, especially vegetarianism.

Rice, lamb, yogurt, ghee (clarified butter), condensed milk, chutneys and chickpeas are common ingredients.

The most important aspect of Indian cuisine is the use and blending of spices. A popular barbecuing technique is performed in a Tandoori oven. Flat bread is also a staple of the Indian diet.

Figure 32: Tandoori Oven

AFRICAN

North African

Known as the "cuisine of the desert," North African cooking is based on cereals, vegetables, dried fruits and grilled meats. Food is served in abundance and is eaten with the fingers, which is inspired by the Koran.

In Algeria and Tunisia the dishes are highly spiced, while Morocco uses more dried lemons for seasoning. Spit roasting and stewing are the common cooking techniques. The best-known North African culinary treat is couscous, which is either combined with meat and vegetables or served sweet with fresh fruit.

Figure 33: Spit Roasting

South African

Figure 34: Stews

This cuisine is inspired by the Dutch, English, French, Indian, Malay and Chinese.

The staple diet is cornmeal, stews and sausages. South Africa is a meat eating country, although seafood is also very important.

The tomatoes, gooseberries and tangerines are famous worldwide. Wine production is also gaining popularity, as are the cookies, cakes, breads and tarts.

MIDDLE EASTERN

The cuisine of the Middle East is diverse, while having some degree of similarity. There are common dishes found throughout this region and some common ingredients include olives, pita bread, honey, Tahini (sesame paste), mint and parsley.

A roasted and mashed eggplant dish called Baba Ghanoush, grilled and skewered meats, called Shish Kabob, hummus (made from chickpeas), and Fattoush, a peasant-style salad made with toasted pita, cucumber, mint and tomatoes are some common dishes.

Figure 35: Shish Kabob

Arab Influence

Arab cuisine dominates this region and is heavily influenced by the muslim religion. There are also some similarities and common techniques taht are borrowed from Indian cuisine.

Lamb and poutry are the most commonly used proteins versus pork, which is forbidden in the Muslim diet, as is alcohol. Coffee and tea are very popular beverages.

Rice is often served with the dishes of this region as are lentils and chickpeas.

Figure 36: Arab Market

Jewish Influence

Another important region within the Middle East with its own unique cuisine is Israel. Naturally influenced by Jewish dietary law, Jewish festivals and Sabbath laws, Israeli cuisine combines local Middle Eastern and Mediterranean dishes adapted by generations of Jewish immigrants, who have settled here.

Figure 37: Figs (above) and Pomegranates

Along with the staples of olives, hummus, fish, couscous and vegetable salads, modern Israeli chefs combine French cooking techniques and local, "Biblical", ingredients such as pomegranates, figs and honey in their cooking.

SOUTHEAST ASIAN

Figure 38: Variety of Spices

In this region, Vietnam, Laos and Cambodia are heavily influenced by China, while Burma and Thailand are more Indian. Garnished soups with vegetables, noodles and thinly sliced meats are prominent. The most common meats are pork, chicken, crab and shrimp.

Rice is usually an accompaniment to dishes that are generally less elaborate and lighter than those of China. Lychees, mandarins, kumquats, pineapples and mangoes are common fruits. Turnips, cabbage, cucumbers and mushrooms are widely used vegetables. Spices such as lemon balm, ginger, shallots and coriander are used to season dishes.

AMERICAN

The cuisine of the original European pioneers is still prominent in the American culinary heritage, which have been fused with many Indian and Mexican dishes. The Jewish, French, Dutch, Italians, Germans, Blacks and Chinese have also enriched it. In short, the diversity of American cuisine can be described as the "melting pot."

Stewing in one cooking vessel is common throughout the nation and is evident in Creole gumbo, Philadelphia pepper pot, New England boiled dinner and Texan chili con carne. Fish, shellfish, spareribs, hamburgers and T-bone steaks reflect the rustic open-air rituals of grilling.

Figure 39: Pot Stew

Cooking Methods

───────────────── DRY-HEAT ─────────────────

Barbecuing

A method of cooking by which foods are covered and slowly cooked in a pit or on a spit using coals or hardwood as a heat source.

The item is basted with a sauce to keep it moist. Today, a barbecued item is commonly interpreted as food that is grilled and basted with a barbecue sauce.

Figure 40: Barbecue with sauce

Baking

A term referring to foods cooked in an oven. As a general rule, baked items are portion-sized and roasted items are larger than one serving.

Figure 41: Cookies are baked

Broiling

Broiling is similar to grilling except that the heat source is above the product. The broiler or salamander are also commonly used to prepare glazed or Gratinée foods.

Figure 42: Broiling steaks

Deep-Frying

Figure 43: Deep Frying

The objective of deep-frying is to produce a crispy, golden brown exterior, which acts as a barrier between the submerged item and the hot, liquid fat.

Grilling

Figure 44: Grilling

Grilled foods are cooked with an intense heat source located below the item. A metal grate is placed over hot charcoals or hardwood to develop a special flavor and appealing markings.

The juices will be sealed into the food by the smoky, slightly charred crust formed on the surface.

Microwaving

The object is placed in a microwave oven to speed the cooking process.

A microwave cooks by heating the water molecules found in a food item. The product is cooked, but does not brown.

Figure 45: Microwaving

Pan Frying

This method is similar to sautéing, however the amount of fat is greater and the heat is less intense.

Normally, pan-fried foods are coated with batter or breaded and are always served with a separate sauce.

Figure 46: Pan frying

Poeleing

Figure 47: Soften vegetables - Step 1

A technique generally used for white meats and game birds.

First select a variety of vegetables and then soften them along with diced ham in a substantial amount of butter.

Figure 48: Place meat on vegetables - Step 2

Then place the meat on the bed of softened vegetables and cover.

The cooking vessel is then placed in the oven.

Because the meat is covered during cooking, the surface will not achieve the deep brown color of a roasted item, but result in a more delicate product.

Figure 49: Place in the oven - Step 3

The foundation and garnish of the sauce is the vegetables, ham, and pan drippings.

Figure 50: Create sauce from the pan drippings - Step 4

Roasting

Figure 51: Roasting

Roasted foods are oven-cooked in an uncovered pan, resulting in a rich golden crust and a moist interior.

Typically, a sauce is derived from the rendered juices.

Spit Roasting

Figure 52: Spit roasting

Spit roasting is a technique that involves placing the food on a rotating rod and exposed to the heat of an open flame.

This method develops a good crust on all sides and assures an even cooking.

Sautéing

This method cooks food rapidly in a small amount of fat over high heat.

The item must be naturally tender and cut into a relatively small size.

Figure 53: Sauté the item

The quick browning leaves a "fond" on the bottom of the pan, which is typically made into a sauce.

Figure 54: Create a "fond"

Mix desired ingredient to make the sauce.

Figure 55: Make the sauce

Smoking

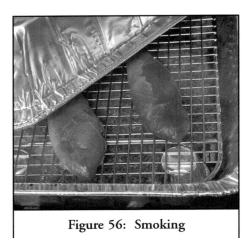

Figure 56: Smoking

This traditional method of preserving fresh food cooks the food by exposing it to the smoke from a wood fire.

Today, smoking is less looked upon as a means of preservation than as a process for giving an appealing flavor to foods. Items may be cold smoked or hot smoked depending on the desired doneness.

Stir-Frying

Figure 57: Stir Frying

Associated with Asian cooking in a wok, stir-frying requires a minimal amount of fat, small pieces of food, and very high heat.

Stir-fried foods must be constantly in motion while being cooked to ensure even doneness. They are usually finished with an intensely flavored sauce.

——— ——— MOIST-HEAT & COMBINATION COOKING ——— ———

Braising

Braising (from the French "braiser"), is a combination cooking method using both moist and dry heat. A successful braise inter-mingles the flavours of the foods being cooked and the cooking liquid. This cooking method dissolves collagen from the meat into gelatin, to enrich and add body to the liquid.

Most braises follow the same basic steps, reviewed here.

First, sear the meat at a high temperature.

If the food does not produce enough liquid of its own, a small amount of vegetables and cooking liquid that often includes an acidic element, such as tomatoes, beer, or wine, is added to the pot, often with stock.

Then cover and cook at a low simmer for a long period of time, until the meat is fork tender.

The sauce is typically derived from the liquid in which the item was cooked.

This method is often used for naturally tougher items; the slow cooking develops flavor and tenderizes the food by breaking down their fibers.

Figure 58: Braising - Step 1

Figure 59: Braising - Step 2

Figure 60: Braising - Step 3

En Papillote

Figure 61: Preparing the Papillote

This method refers to foods that are wrapped tightly in parchment paper and baked in the oven.

The entire package is brought to the table and cut open in front of the customer, who can then enjoy its pleasingly steamed fragrance.

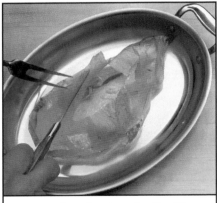

Figure 62: Serving the Papillote

Poaching

Figure 63: Poaching Salmon

Poaching an item allows it to be cooked gently by submerging it in a flavorful liquid. The item is removed when cooked and always served with a separate sauce.

Shallow-Poaching

This method cooks food rapidly in a small amount of fat over high heat.

The item must be naturally tender and cut into a relatively small size.

Figure 64: Shallow poach

Simmering and Boiling

These methods cook a wide variety of foods in a liquid that is at a light simmer or rolling boil.

Some examples are pasta, dried beans, boiled beef and lobster.

Figure 65: Boiling lobster

Sous Vide

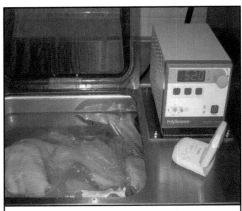

Figure 66: Sous Vide

Sous vide, French for "under vacuum", is a method that involves placing an item in an air-tight plastic bag and then cooking the item slowly in a water bath that is generally maintained at an unusually low temperature.

Unlike boiling or simmering the water, which occurs at or around 212 degrees Fahrenheit, the water bath is kept at an average temperature of 140 degrees. The sous vide item is held at this temperature for an extended period of time -- occasionally for as long as 24 to 48 hours.

This technique may be used to tenderize a tough cut of meat, such as beef short ribs, as a substitute for the long, slow braising method.

Steaming

Steaming is achieved by surrounding the product in vapor.

The food is placed in a covered vessel with a perforated bottom and set over boiling stock or water.

This method is an exceptional way to retain a food's flavor, shape, texture and many of the vitamins and minerals.

Figure 67: Steaming broccoli

Stewing

The technique of placing bite-sized foods barely covered with a liquid to simmer slowly in a covered pot for a long period of time. All the flavors then blend together nicely.

Figure 68: Stewing

Cooking Temperatures

Every day, misunderstandings concerning the communication of cooking temperatures between customers, the wait staff, and the kitchen cost establishments significant losses.

These losses are measured in:
- Waste of product
- Loss of production time
- A spoiled experience for guests
- Tarnishing the professional reputation of the establishment

Personal preferenece of the guest and occasionally the cut of the item determines its cooking temperature.

Communicating the correct internal temperature is not only important from a food safety perspective, but also from a customer satification viewpoint. Below we describe each of the main categories of temperatures, using beef in photographic examples.

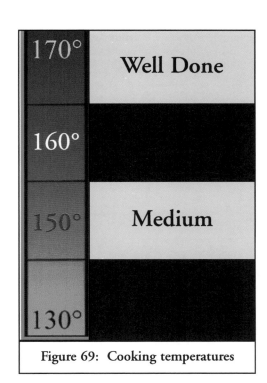

Figure 69: Cooking temperatures

Blue

Achieved by just barely searing the flesh, leaving the center cool.

In order to properly cook meat to blue, it should remain at room temperature to take off the chill, therefore making it vulnerable from a sanitation perspective.

Figure 70: Meat cooked Blue

Figure 71: Rare cooking

Medium Rare

Center of the item is 140 degrees.

The color will change to a more pinkish color and will still be very juicy.

Rare

Center of the item is 130 degrees.

The meat will be a deep red with free running blood, but warm throughout.

Figure 72: Medium Rare cooking

Medium

Center of the item is 150 degrees.

The meat will be a light pink color.

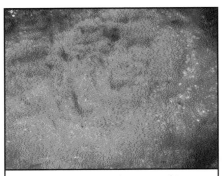

Figure 73: Medium cooking

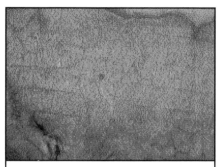

Figure 74: Medium Well cooking

Medium Well

Center of the item is 160 degrees. Only a hint of pink should remain.

Well Done

Center of the item is 170 degrees.

There should be no pink color or free running juices.

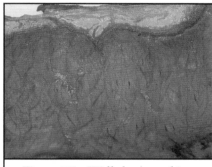

Figure 75: Well done cooking

Vegetable Cuts

Different types of cuts can add drama and flair to any dish. If you want to impress your friends and Chef, there are a few formal cuts and names that are worth learning.

Figure 76: Dice cut

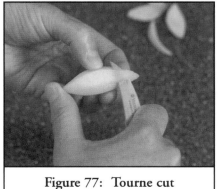

Figure 77: Tourne cut

————————— VEGETABLE CUTS COMPARISON —————————

The secret to make professional looking vegetables is, within a style, to make them all look the same with neat edges.

As the method to create most cuts are quite similar, the real key is to know the size of the cut you are attempting to make.

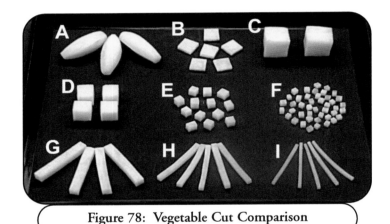

Figure 78: Vegetable Cut Comparison

Tourne (Figure 8-35 Item A)
Approximately two inches with seven sides, and resembles a football. Commonly used for potatoes and root vegetables.

Paysanne / Peasant (Figure 8-35 Item B)
Peasant is usually 1/2"x1/2"x1/8". Generally used to give a rustic or home-style appeal.

Large Dice (Figure 8-35 Item C)
Cubes of the dimension 3/4"x3/4"x3/4".

Medium Dice (Figure 8-35 Item D)
Cubes having the dimensions 1/2"x1/2"x1/2".

Small Dice (Figure 8-35 Item E)
Cubes having the dimensions 1/4"x1/4"x1/4".

Brunoise (Figure 8-35 Item F)
1/8x1/8x/1/8

Batonnet (Figure 8-35 Item G)
Rectangular cuts sized 1/4"x 1/4"x2"

Julienne / Allumette (Figure 8-35 Item H)
Sized 1/8"x1/8"x2".
Allumette usually refers only to potatoes.

Fine Julienne (Figure 8-35 Item I)
Small rectangular cuts sized 1/16"x1/16"x2"

Seafood

Seafood is classified in two broad categories: Fish and Shellfish. Helping customers determine what type of dish they would enjoy, I have found that by asking a few basic questions, such as: "Do you have a preference for fish or crustacean?" "Do you like a flaky or firm fish?" "How do you like having your seafood cooked?" a server can quickly guide a customer to a happy choice. Adding to guests' experience, study the history or details of items on the menu. That way, you can offer insights to a customer who shows interest. You just may improve your check amount along with customer satisfaction.

FISH CATEGORIES

Fish food items are equipped with fins, backbones and gills, and may live in either saltwater or freshwater.

Fish is an excellent source of protein and has a low fat content. They can be divided into three categories, depending on their percentage of fat:

• Lean fish (0.5-4%) will have a mild flesh and a light color. Fish in this category are cod, flounder, grouper, haddock, hake, black sea bass, halibut, pollack, pike, red snapper, rockfish, and tilefish. Poaching and Sautéing are good methods for lean fish.

• Semi-oily or Moderate-fat fish (4.1-10%) include sardines, mullet, herring, trout, catfish, bass, sword fish and whiting.

• Oily or High-fat fish can reach up to 30% fat, but the common is about 12%. The fat gives the flesh a darker color, firmer texture and more distinctive flavor. Eel, salmon, tuna, smelt, mackerel and sturgeon fit this category, and are great for grilling.

Flat Fish

In the flat fish group, there are some excellent eating fish. Flat fish are generally non-aggressive, bottom dwellers that only swim when necessary. Included in this category are Halibut, Turbot, and Dover Sole.

Halibut can be found in the deep waters of the North Atlantic. It has white, firm flesh that can be used in various cooking methods but is best when sautéed, baked, poached, or used in chowders. Like Halibut, Turbot is another firm, white-fleshed fish that also can be used in various

Figure 79: Flat Fish

cooking methods. It is best when poached, sautéed or baked. Unlike the Halibut, the Turbot is found in the Mediterranean and is now farmed raised around the world.

Although, as per its name, the "Dover" Sole is most prized when from the English channel, it is one of the most valued flat fish in the world. It is found throughout European waters, including the Mediterranean. It has a delicate, white flesh with a small flake and sweet flavor. Dover Sole is best when baked or grilled whole, sautéed, or poached.

Figure 80: Dover Sole

Round Fish

These fish are round to oval, and have flesh ranging from white to dark. The backbone runs along the back creating a filet on both sides. When viewed in its cross section, the body of the round fish goes from truly round to somewhat flat. Some round fishes are more aggressive than others; which is why the flesh of round fish varies in color from white to dark. If a fish's flesh is white, it is less aggressive and a slow swimmer. But if the flesh is medium to dark in color, it means the fish is more active and has a higher fat content.

Figure 81: Round Fish

Atlantic Salmon is one of numerous salmons being used in this family of high-fat content fish. Although this fish has virtually disappeared from North Atlantic rivers in the wild, it has been domesticated in order to provide the commercial market all year long. Atlantic Salmon is a firm, fatty fish that can be sautéed, grilled, baked, smoked and poached. The domesticated Atlantic Salmon can be found in the United States, Europe, and South America.

Although the Striped Bass is not as fatty as the Atlantic Salmon, it is just as versatile. Striped Bass is found from the State of New York to the Carolinas on the east coast of the U.S. and from western Canada down to the State of California. Fisherman use long fishing lines and gill nets to capture this medium-active fish. When raw, its flesh is gray in color, and when cooked fresh, this fish has a large, firm flaky texture and a sweet mild flavor.

Like salmon, Striped Bass is a firm fish, so most of the cooking techniques used with salmon will be suitable for this fish as well.

Another fish that looks similar to Striped Bass, but is not, is Hybrid Striped Bass. Hybrid Striped Bass is being farm-raised in the U.S., by crossbreeding the Striped Bass and the fresh water White Bass. You can tell these two fish apart by looking very closely. The stripes on the skin of the hybrid are broken, as in dashed, and are generally not as big as those of the Striped Bass. For flavor and taste, most people prefer Striped Bass over its hybrid counterpart, in part because the hybrid has a tendency to be distinctly less flavorful and can even be flavorless.

Striped Bass is a prized fish, but it is not as

important as the Atlantic Cod, however. The Atlantic Cod is known as the fish that changed the world. This fish was not only a staple food for Europeans, but was a staple food for the new world as well. Early settlers in the New World and Canada depended on this fish not only for food for long journeys, but for commerce, trade,

Figure 82: Striped Bass

and work. The cod stocks were so abundant from the late 1800's to the late 1970's that each fisherman caught nothing less than 50 pounds per day. even though Atlantic Cod is not as prevalent as it once was, this fish still remains a staple in the fishing industry and prepared in kitchens and restaurants around the world.

Cod can be salted and dried, or made into processed fish sticks. Also, the cheeks and tongues can be used in various cooking methods such as broiled, grilled, sautéed, pan fried, poached, deep fried, steamed. Cod livers are used for vitamin A and D nutritional supplements, as dietary and health aids.

Cod is a low activity, ground fish typically found off the northeastern coast of the United States and Canada by fishermen who trap, trawl, and use gill netting to catch them. Its flesh is white with a large delicate flake; it has a mineral earthy flavor at times that is not strong. Cod is a very versatile and neutral fish that can be used in various cooking methods. Relatives of the cod family,

Figure 83: Monkfish

which are sometimes substituted in recipes, include Haddock, Pollack, Hake, and Cusk. Each has a texture and taste similar to cod.

Another low to medium activity Round

Fishes are Black Sea Bass, Monkfish, Red Snapper, Sablefish, and John Dory. The Black Sea Bass is a white-fleshed fish found from Florida to Long Island. The flesh is firm; the flavor distinctive and it is best when grilled, fried whole or sautéed with the skin on.

The Monkfish, or Anglerfish, is an ugly fish. It has a huge head with a fishing-rod-like antenna protruding from its head and that it uses to entice and capture its meals. The only usable part of the monkfish is the tail; the head is usually discarded at sea. The Monkfish's meat is firm, white, and sweet with no flake. It provides the best flavor when roasted or sautéed, but can be baked, pan fried, or used in soups.

Black Cod or Sablefish is a favorite that can be found in North American waters. It has a sweet, buttery flavor that gives it a very pronounced and succulent taste. Because of its high fat content, sablefish can be sautéed, steamed, baked, smoked, or grilled. Red Snapper can be found around reefs in the Gulf of Mexico and Florida and even as far north as Massachusetts. Red Snapper has a large and delicate flake. Like the Black Sea Bass, the Red Snapper can be sautéed, baked, or grilled and has a mild and delicate flavor.

Another favorite is the John Dory, or St. Peters fish. According to Claus Frimodt, it is said "to be the legacy of St. Peter who took the tribute from the mouth of the fish, leaving the mark of his thumb on the species." John Dory are usually located in the waters of the Mediterranean, New Zealand, Australia, and South Africa. Its flesh is white, sweet, and firm. The John Dory is very versatile and can be used in various cooking methods, but is best when sautéed.

Finishing up this discussion on round fish are three very active and aggressive swimmers, which are known for their excellent fighting and eating qualities--not only in food industry but also in the sport fishing world. They are: Swordfish, Mahi-Mahi and Tuna.

Swordfish are found worldwide and are very aggressive. Matching its aggressive nature is its large size and a good dose of

Figure 84: Swordfish kabobs

Figure 85: Mahi-Mahi

strength. So much so that this fish sometimes has to be harpooned by fisherman to get it aboard. Depending on where the fish is caught the flesh can range from a pinkish color to tan, but don't be alarmed to see either as the difference is due to its diet. Swordfish is a firm fish with no flake. It can be used in soups, but is best when grilled, baked, or sautéed.

Another highly aggressive fish, but beautiful when alive is Mahi-Mahi. Besides having stunning colors, it is known for its firm, mild, and sweet flavor. Originally from Hawaii, it can be located offshore in almost any warm water area. Like the swordfish, is best grilled, broiled, or sautéed.

The last aggressive, high-active species discussed here is Tuna. Although there are

Figure 86: Seared Tuna

eight different species in this family, I focus here on the three that are widely used interchangeably because they have the same eating qualities. Blue Fin is the largest of the family found in the western Atlantic. It has a high fat content, pink to red firm flesh, and is used mainly for sashimi, but can be grilled or sautéed. Bigeye is the second largest of the family found in the warm, sub-tropical waters of the Atlantic and the Pacific. Its flesh is firm and a little lighter in color than the Blue Fin. The Bigeye can also be grilled, pan-seared or used for sashimi. Although the Yellow Fin tuna is smaller than either the Blue Fin or Bigeye, it is still a prized fish that is also found in warm tropical waters and has the same eating and cooking qualities as both Blue Fin and Bigeye.

Non-bony Fish

Figure 87: Shark

This category of fish have cartilage rather than bones. These include shark, skate and ray.

There are numerous delicious receipes for shark, but it is suggested to soak in milk overnight prior to preparing it in a dish.

There are also various species of shark, some of which may be protected. So ensure you know which kind you can fix for dinner and which one you need to let go.

--- FISH PRESENTATIONS ---

Pan Dressed

A portion sized fish that has had the entrails, scales, tail and fins removed. It may have the head on or off.

Figure 88: Pan dressed

Steaks

A cross-section cut of a larger fish that will contain a small piece of backbone.

Figure 89: Steak cut

Filet

A boneless, lengthwise cut of fish that is sliced from the sides. The skin may or may not be removed.

Figure 90: Salmon Filet

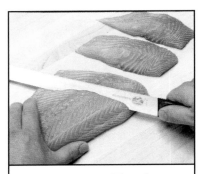

Figure 91: Tranche

Tranche

A portion cut on a 45 degree angle from a thick filet.

Figure 92: Goujonette

Goujonette

Small, thin strips of filet, resembling cigars in their shape.

They are typically breaded and fried.

Figure 93: Paupiette

Paupiette

Thin, rolled filets that are usually spread with a stuffing to keep it a tight round spiral.

Shallow poaching is the most common technique for this preparation.

CAVIAR

Caviar is considered one of life's luxuries. Caviar is procured mostly from the aspian Sea where Russians and Iranians share the main fishing areas. Three ex-Soviet countries, Azerbaïdjan, Kazakhstan and Turkmenistan, also exploit it. Divided into three basins, the Caspian is the world's largest enclosed sea. The northern basin which is quite shallow, a central one about 175 meters deep and a southern one are where the best sturgeons for caviar production are to be found.

The main Russian fishing area is situated in the North next to the Volga delta where 75% of the Caspian fishing is done. Before the revolution, the fishing concessions were granted by the czar.

Production is now under the control of one state body, the V/O Prodintorg. In the 60's, the building of dams on the Volga put some of the sturgeon species like the beluga in jeopardy as they used to swim up this river to spawn. To balance this problem, hatchling sturgeons were released by the Russian government but the dismantlement of the Soviet block and the emergence of new countries with no fishing or polution regulations has increased the problems.

The Iranians fish on the southern area where the water is the deepest. Up to the Iranian revolution by the Imam Komeyni,

fishing production was almost all under Russian control.

The process to make caviar is relatively simple: The eggs are removed from the fish while it is still alive. The roe accounts for about 15 to 18 percent of the fish. The caviar is immediately put trough a mesh to remove all the surrounding membrane. It is then cleaned and put on draining racks usually made of horse's hair. According to the color, size, smell and taste, it will be decided if the eggs are to be first or second quality, pressed or pasteurised. The caviar is then mixed with salt and borax. Salt preserves the eggs and borax takes away some of the saltiness (caviar buyers specify the amount, usually 4 to 10 percent salt to 0.5 percent borax). The quality of the salt is extremely important; it is generally collected and dried several years before using to remove the chlorine it naturally contains.

Figure 94: Caviar on Mother-of-pearl

The distinction between the types of caviar is by the different species of sturgeons as follows:

Beluga - From Huso Huso, the largest sturgeon. It can weigh up to 1000Kg and has such a large mouth that it is able to swallow whole salmon. Beluga caviar is grey to black, the greyer the better, and the fish is the only species that is exclusively carnivorous. It is also the most expensive due to his rarity. To tell you have Beluga caviar, squeeze an egg and you should see a clear white oil coming out. Beluga is generally sold in blue tins or with a blue mark.

Oscietra - It's delicate taste with a nutty flavour makes it the best caviar. Oscietra (Acipenser guelden staedti) can weigh up to 80Kg. It is oscietra that provides the very rare golden caviar (it comes from older fish). To tell you have ocietra, squeeze an egg and you should see yellowish oil coming out. It is usually sold in yellow tins or with a yellow mark.

Sevruga - From Acipencer stellatus the main source, it is the less expensive of Caspian caviar. The eggs are smaller, blacker and saltier than the other types.

Malossol - The only word that refers to technique rather than species, meaning lightly salted and indicating caviar of particular excellence from fish caught at the beginning of the season.

Pressed Caviar or Paiousnaia - The ripest sevruga eggs, taken at the end of the season are processed to make a block which has a stronger flavour that can be served with chopped onions, hard boiled egg whites and yolks (sampled separately), parsley and blinis with cream.

The best way to appreciate caviar is to place a small quantity on the tip of the tongue and crush the eggs against the palate to release their subtle flavour. A neutral accompaniment like very thin toast or blinis and a delicate unsalted butter or sour cream can be served with caviar.

Figure 95: Caviar with Pancakes

The tradition is that you drink iced vodka with caviar but Champagne brut goes very well with it also.

Finally, the eggs help metabolize the alcohol as they contain formique acid. Which explains why we can abundantly drink vodka while enjoying caviar. The vodka's neutral taste also explains the tradition of using this particular alcohol.

There is nothing simpler than serving caviar as long as you respect a few rules:

□ For the consumption and the handling of caviar never use silverware. It reacts and tastes metallic. Always use bone, gold or china.

□ Allow 30 to 50gr per person. It is preferable to serve caviar from the tin itself (the tin contains information such as the number of fish, how many tins were produced with the same roe and the classification of the eggs colour).

Figure 96: Caviar Appetizer

Figure 97: Flying Fish Roe on Sushi

□ Otherwise use a china, glass or crystal container. Remove the tin from the refrigerator and place in crushed ice 15 minutes before serving (to allow the aromas to develop).

□ Present the tin open set in crushed iced with the lid on the side.

□ Accompaniments such as black pepper, lemon, onion or herbs should be avoided or reserved for pressed caviar.

--- SHELLFISH ---

Besides the numerous varieties of round and flat fish, there are just as many delicious varieties of shellfish and crustaceans.

The shellfish category includes all invertebrate aquatic animals that have a shell of some kind.

Crustaceans

Figure 98: Crustaceans

Crustaceans are shellfish that have jointed legs and exo-skeletons. Shrimp, Lobsters, Crabs, and Crawfish are considered crustaceans. Crustaceans have some similarity in taste and texture. When fresh, a crustaceans' flesh is mild, sweet and firm. All species can be steamed, poached, sautéed, or used in soups.

Small crustaceans can be served whole or in the form of a tail, while larger ones are also shelled into the claws, trunks and legs.

Mollusks

Figure 99: Octopus

Mollusks are divided into three groups: Gastropods or Univalves are single shelled animals such as snails, conch and abalone. Bivalves like clams, mussels, scallops and oysters are commonly served in their hinged shell.

Cephalopods include octopus, cuttlefish and squid. Their tentacles are attached to their heads and they have an ink sac, which is used to evade predators.

The most common shellfish are oysters, mussels, and scallops.

Oysters usually get their flavor from the water where they live and are harvested. Some popular varieties are Belon, Wellfleet, Apalachicola, and Kumamoto.

Scallops are generally known for their sweet, firm texture, and are categorized as either Bay Scallops or Sea Scallops.

Bay Scallops are the smaller of the two varieties and tend to be sweeter. Both types are great grilled, broiled, sautéed, deep fried, or even raw.

Finally, Mussels are many cultivated in Maine but can also be found adhering to

Figure 100: Shrimp and Mussels

rocks and piers on both U.S. coastlines. Mussels have fresh, clean sea flavor when fresh.

Figure 101: Seafood Market

Meats

People have been eating meat since the time of the caveman. The word meat means any of the edible parts of a carcass. Some cuts of meat are naturally very tender while others must be braised for a long period of time to become palatable.

There are four general categories of meat:
- White Meat,
- Dark or Game Meat,
- Offal (Organ) Meat, and
- Red Meat.

MEAT CATEGORIES

White Meats

Veal and pork make up this category. Veal has a delicate flavor and fine texture. True veal will have a creamy white meat that is barely tinged with pink, due to its young age. Moist heat cooking methods are sometimes preferred to make up for the lack of natural fat. Pork, on the other hand, is rather high in fat, but improved feeding techniques have lowered this dramatically. The domesticated pig is eaten fresh, smoked, cured and salted.

Recently a high-end pork has found its way to market. It's called the Kurobuta, from pure-bread Berkshire pigs. Kurobuta literally means 'black pig' in Japanese, and in the US it is generally referred to American Kurobuta or Certified Berkshire. Just as with Kobe beef, Kurobuta or Berkshire pigs are raised under very strict conditions of diet and even exercise as these pigs are allowed plenty of roaming space. Their natural diets are often supplemented with apples, alfalfa and milk to promote sweeter and cleaner flavors in the meat. Antibiotics and growth-hormones are forbidden, thus allowing the animal to grow as naturally and as stress-free as possible.

Berkshire pigs are genetically predisposed to producing the finest quality of pork. Its meat is generally darker in color and may be consumed on the rare side of medium, much to the dismay of those who are still weary of Trichinosis. The clean environment in which these animals are raised is far superior to the common practices unfortunately seen on the majority of the market, removing the concern of illness.

Figure 102: Berkshire pig

Dark or Game Meats

Game animals' flesh may be pale in color or a rich ruby red, and may have a delicate to gamy flavor.

Venison, wild boar, moose, bear, rabbit and elk will offer tasty meat with less cholesterol and fat than beef.

Figure 103: Elk

Offal (Organ) Meats

Organ meat include such items as the brain, liver, stomach, kidneys, tongue and heart of the animal.

There are many different ways to prepare and serve items in this category, including pan frying and stewing.

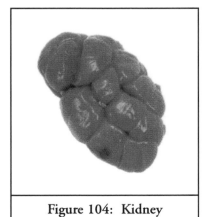

Figure 104: Kidney

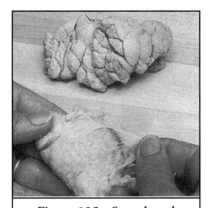

Figure 105: Sweetbread

Red Meats

Lamb and beef fall into this category. Lamb has been looked upon as having a "musty" taste, but improved methods for raising sheep have helped this. When a sheep turns one year of age is labeled mutton, which is slightly tougher and develop in its flavor.

Beef is the meat of a bovine (cow) that is more than one year of age. And while there are many breed of bovine, other factors that influence overall taste of the beef include how the cattle was raised, the amount of fat in the meat, the cut, and its processing.

One method of processing is known as "aged beef." This term means that the meat is held uncovered, in a meat locker to increase its tenderness and give it a more pronounced flavor.

MEAT CUTS BY PRIMAL AREA

For the dining room staff, understanding where a piece of meat is cut from will assist in answering questions from customers. First, there are nine major areas, or "Primals" represented. Generally speaking, almost anything that is not from the center top area of the animal can be used for stew beef or ground beef, *but,* if the chef is careful, there are very useful cuts in all areas.

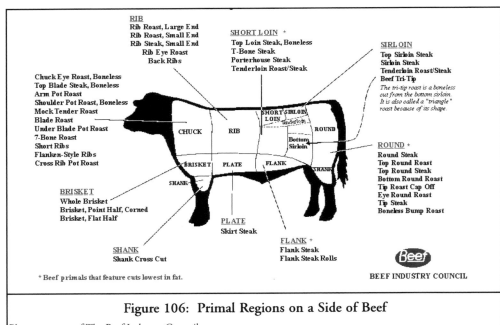

Figure 106: Primal Regions on a Side of Beef

Photo courtesy of The Beef Industry Council

The Chuck

One of the biggest of all the sections, the Chuck is in essence the shoulder of the beast. Used for large roasts, many different styles of slow-cooked roasts and stew meats, anything that says "blade" (referring to the shoulder blade), and a slightly nicer ground beef labeled "ground chuck."

This is where the relatively new and very popular "Flat Iron" comes from. The Flat Iron was hidden inside the more complicated larger muscles, and as the second most tender cut has become the fashionable steak in the last ten years.

The Brisket

The front "chest" area (like the steer's "pecs"), the brisket is fairly famous for dishes named after itself. Not a complex primal, this area is fairly straight forward. Brisket is most famous for it's use in Texas Barbecue and corned beef, but any long term braising or smoking can produce an amazing product by breaking down the many fibers and connective tissues into juicy flavor. A brine or a marinade is well received, and the long fibers absorb it well.

The Shank

One of the smallest sections, this is basically the cross-cut of the legs. Famous for its use in an Italian dish called Osso Bucco, the shank is more often ground into hamburger or cut into stew meat. Like Oxtails, which are in fact Beef Cattle tails, shanks are not a popular as other cuts.

Please note that Shank and Tail, when properly braised can be some of the best food produced by cattle due to the large amount of connective tissue and gelatins that can break down and create flavor and texture not possible in leaner more "grill-ready" steaks.

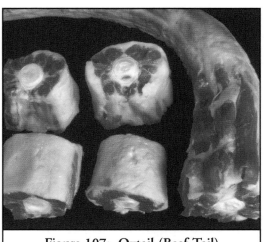

Figure 107: Oxtail (Beef Tail)

The Plate

The lower chest area below the ribs, this is often opened during disembowment and is not super meaty. Often there are short ribs here which if properly braised can make for legendary cuisine.

Although not shown on the Beef Council's Diagram, this is the location of the "Hanger Steak" (also known as "hanging tender") which is part of the diaphragm inside the skirt and can be very tender and delicious due to its proximity to the kidneys.

The Hanger Steak was also once called the Butcher's Steak due to the fact that there is only one per animal and the butchers used to keep this cut for themselves.

In most usage, skirt steak has a lot in common with flank steak and both are fairly tough if improperly used, but take very well to marinades and are used very often in ethic cuisines from Mexican to Chinese to Indian Curry.

The Flank

Figure 108: London Broil

An even smaller area behind the skirt and always opened up into big flaps, this area is known for "flank steak", which is flat with long fibers and perfect for uses like fajitas and Chinese stir fry.

A very popular dish from the post-war era utilizing this cut or perhaps some types of sirloin was called "London Broil", a housewife's favorite meant to be cooked very quickly under a very hot broiler and sliced against the grain.

The Round

The very large area of the rear hind quarter, this section is used for large roasts, stew meat, ground beef. It is an area of much discussion as many of the sub-sections can be used as substitutes for almost anything from fajita meat to chicken fried steak to London broil. A lot of wonderful stews can be made from this area, and there are many types of less expensive steaks like "round steak" and "top round". On a scale of 1-10 these steaks would be a 4, less tender than the worst sirloin, but usually better than the flank and skirt options. Pounding it out for Chicken Fried Steaks and cutting into meaty chunks for stews are good cooking options. This cut can also be used for fine dining through the "Paillard." Thinly sliced and pounded out, this elite version of chicken fried steak can take wonderful sauces from soubise to demi-glace.

Figure 110: Paillard

Figure 109: Cutlet

Figure 111: Emincé

The Rib

The Rib Primal gives us not only beef ribs, which carry more meat and a deeper flavor than the pork version, but also this is the area from which we cut the bone-in or boneless rib roast, also known as "Prime Rib".

If cut into individual steaks, this roast, or prime rib, is simply "ribeye steak". It is the ribeyes protected area and higher fat levels that give it such great flavor and juiciness. If ordering a steak and you do not know the marbling or origin of it, the Ribeye is a excellent choice.

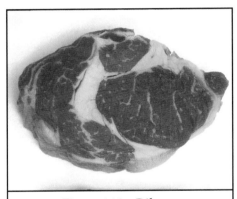

Figure 112: Rib eye

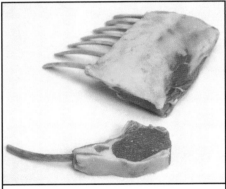

Figure 113: Rack of Lamb

The Sirloin

This area is between the round and the shortloin which contains the very best meat. With such proximity to the Short Loin, there is a great deal of quality here, but the area is amazingly flexible; producing cuts not much better than round or chuck or some of the best steaks at the best prices. The legend says that this cut was knighted by a British Lord, hence the name "Sir" Loin, and if you get a very good piece you will know why.

This is the location of the fairly hip and popular "tri-tip" or "tip" steak, as well as the many forms of sirloin, top sirloin, and mock tenders. Other uses for the sirloin include creating better examples of lower quality dishes such as "ground sirloin" for the best burgers, or "pounded sirloin" for the best Chicken Fried Steak or "sirloin strips" for the best stir fry or fajitas. Among the primals, the Sirloin is perhaps the most flexible and commonly used by a wide variety of restaurants.

The Short Loin

If there is a King of the Primal Areas, there is no argument that it is the Short Loin. It is the center of the animal, and it is from this region that we get the very best steaks in the world. In very serious steakhouses, it is this primal you will see darkening in their dry-aging room. Filet Mignon, New York Strip, T-Bones, and Porterhouses all come from the short loin. There are two very distinct ways to cut a loin for a restaurant.

The first is to remove the main muscles leaving the bone behind. This separates the piece into a tenderloin and a strip loin.

When trimmed down these form two of the three most famous steaks: the Filet Mignon (from the tenderloin) and the New York Strip (from the strip loin).

These long sub-primals come from cutting "lengthwise" off the bone. You can also cut across the bone, and this leaves a piece of bone shaped roughly like a "T" with a piece of tenderloin or filet mignon on one side and a piece of strip loin or new york strip on the other side. This cross-cut steak with a piece of both is called a "T-Bone". If cross-cut the bone in the very best part of the Short Loin and the filet section is very large, this is the ultimate steak, and it is called a Porterhouse. Over the years, other variations, such as bone-in filets and bone-in strips were developed.

Figure 114: New York Strip

Figure 115: T-Bone

Poultry and Game Birds

POULTRY

Poultry is any domesticated bird used as food, and is a highly nutritional complete protein. Chicken is by far the most popular bird desired for both its meat and eggs. Chicken may fall into several classifications depending on its age, size and the method used to raise it. Poussin (spring chicken) is a 4-6 week old chicken and is typically roasted whole. Rock Cornish hens are miniature chickens under 2½ pounds.

A Capon is a rooster that is castrated while young. They have flavorful, tender and juicy meat that is best when roasted. "Free-range" means that the bird was raised with more than one square foot of space and was allowed freedom to roam outside. Mass-pro-

duced birds will have a very delicate flavored, white flesh, while the increased activity of free-range birds offer darker meat and more pronounced flavor. Since neither bird is allowed to fly the breast will be lighter in color than the leg and thigh meat. Turkey or hen (female) have a more distinct flavor than chicken and are much larger.

Young geese are called goslings, and young ducks are called ducklings. The meat is darker in color and higher in fat than most domesticated birds. While young, these birds are suitable for all cooking methods, however when older it is best to braise or stew them. Another cooking method for the legs and thighs is known as confit, which means to salt the meat and slowly cook it in its own fat until tender.

Geese and duck are also highly prized for their livers, or Foie Gras. Foie Gras is the fattened liver of force-fed duck and geese; it is usually sautéed or served cold as a terrine or mousse.

The three main breeds of duck in America are the Peking, Muscovy and Mulard. The Mulard is actually a crossbreed between the Peking and Muscovy duck and is mostly used for Foie Gras production in this country. A squab is a young domesticated pigeon that has never been allowed to fly. The meat is dark and extremely tender. The Guinea Hen is closely related to the squab.

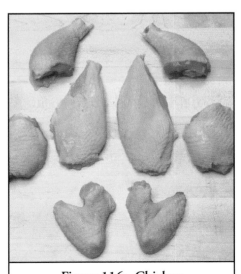

Figure 116: Chicken

GAME BIRDS

Any wild bird suitable to eat is a game bird. They are much leaner than domesticated birds and will have a gamy flavor that becomes more intense with age. Older game birds are best cooked with slow, moist heat. A quail is the smallest of the game birds and is usually stuffed and roasted whole. Pheasants are a meaty bird that may be farm-raised resulting in a much less gamy flavor. Other game birds include partridge, woodcock, wild duck, wild turkey and thrush.

Figure 117: Pheasant

CUTS

Magret

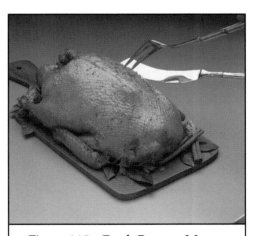

Figure 118: Duck Breast - Magret

This is the portion of the meat from the breast of a duck. Traditionally, this was reserved specifically for ducks that were used for Foie Gras production.

Supreme or French Cut

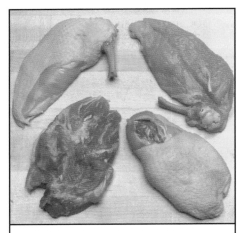

Figure 119: Chicken - Supreme or French Cut

A breast that is served with the first wing joint left attached.

Aiguillette

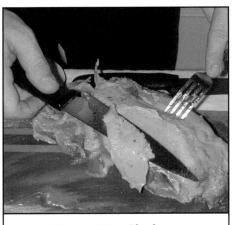

Figure 120: Chicken - Aiguillette Cut

A French term for a thin slice of breast meat.

Stocks, Soups and Sauces

STOCKS

Stocks are a flavorful liquid prepared by slowly simmering bones, vegetables and other flavor enhancing ingredients in water.

They are used as a foundation for several kitchen applications, namely soups and sauces. There are two different types of stocks: White and Brown.

White Stock

White stock is made from the bones of veal, beef, fish or poultry. This neutral flavored liquid is used for contributing body and a light flavor to an item.

The procedure for making white stock differs from that of brown stock mainly in that rather than roasting the bones beforehand, they are blanched instead.

Blanching helps get rid of the impurities in the bones that can cloud the stock.

Herbs and spices (bay leaf, thyme, black peppercorns are examples) are added to stock in one of two ways:
1) Individually, or
2) Prepared in a bundle, or "bouquet garni."

Figure 121: Ingredients for White Stock using Chicken

Figure 122: Cooking White Stock

Brown Stock

Like white stock, brown stock has an extremely important role in cooking. It is indispensable and always on hand in all fine professional kitchens.

Brown stock requires that the meaty bones are first roasted in an oven until they develop a deep caramel color.

Vegetables and a tomato product are also browned in hot fat to add color and complexity to the finished brown stock.

Constantly stir the tomato paste during cooking, until it turns a brick red color. Cooking the tomato paste removes its sharp acidity and will deepen the color of the finished stock.

Classically, brown stock is made using a mixture of veal meat and bones. The meat adds flavor while the bones contribute flavor and gelatin, which will give the finished stock consistency. Brown veal stock is widely used for preparing sauces.

Figure 123: Ingredients for Brown Stock using Veal Bones

Figure 124: Cooking the tomato paste

—————— OTHER COOKING LIQUIDS ——————

Broth or Bouillon

Bouillon is very similar to a stock although more flavorful due to actual pieces of meat and not just bones simmered in the liquid.

Figure 125: Cup of Bouillon

Vegetable Broth

This broth is simply made by cooking peeled and cleaned vegetables in water. The vegetables may also first be lightly browned (caramelized) in hot oil as to develop a richer flavor. This is popular in vegetarian cooking.

Court Bouillon

Also called "short broth," this Bouillon is an acidic liquid primarily used for cooking fish and vegetables.

Wine, vinegar or citrus juice give this light vegetable broth its character.

Figure 126: Court Bouillon

Consommé

This crystal clear, intensely flavored stock is clarified by egg white protein and refortified by ground meat. It is variously used as a soup, sauce base or cold savory jelly.

Figure 127: Consommé

Glazes

Glazes are stocks that have been reduced to a syrupy consistency. They are used primarily for finishing sauces to add a brilliant shine and powerful flavor.

Fumet or Essence

Fumets are commonly made from fish, mushrooms or other highly flavored ingredients.

It is essentially a concentrated stock highlighting a particular ingredient.

Figure 128: Ingredients for Fumet

THICKENERS

Thickeners are added to soups and sauces to provide additional body. "Slurry" is a starch (cornstarch or arrowroot) dissolved in a cold liquid. The result is a creamy solution that quickly thickens a boiling liquid. On the other hand, "roux" must be cooked for a longer period of time.

A combination made by slowly cooking fat and flour, there are three types of roux. White roux and blonde roux are made with butter, and are used to thicken cream and white sauces and light soups. A brown roux may be made with rendered meat fat or oil and is used not only as a thickener, but also for contributing a nutty flavor from its toasted flour.

Figure 129: Creating a Roux

Figure 130: Types of Roux

A "Beurre-Manié" is basically an uncooked roux that is used to quickly thicken sauces and add a nice shine.

Another thickener that is used for its smooth texture and golden shine is a "Liaison." This egg yolk and cream mixture, which is also sometimes made with the addition of slurry, can enrich a finished soup or sauce.

It is also common to replace the heavy cream with sour cream or crème fraîche. Sour cream will add an acidic, tangy characteristic, while crème fraîche offers a nutty flavor and velvety rich texture.

--------------------------------- SOUPS ---------------------------------

Broth and Consommé

Described earlier in 'Other Cooking Liquids', these liquids may be served as soups by simply adding a garnish of vegetables or other items.

Figure 131: Consommé Soup

Thick Soups

Thick soups are those that use a thickening agent. This categroy is further sub-divided by the thickening agent and their method of preparation.

Cream Soups

As the name suggests, Cream Soups are those made from milk thickened with roux and finished with cream. The flavoring ingredients are cooked in the liquid, puréed and strained to achieve a rich smooth soup. Typically, a garnish that reflects the major flavoring ingredient is added just before service.

Figure 132: Cream Soup

Cooked with flavoring ingredient

Puréed and Strained

Garnished

Velouté Soups

This white stock is thickened with roux and finished with a liaison.

The same garnish scenario for cream soups applies to Velouté soups.

Figure 133: Velouté Soup

Purée Soups

Purée soups are those soups that are thickened by starch contained in the vegetables or beans cooked in it.

This soup will have a coarser texture because it is not strained.

Figure 134: Beans used as the thickening agent

Figure 135: Puréed in Pot

Bisque

Traditionally made from crustaceans, bisque is thickened with puréed rice. Today, there are vegetable-based bisques thickened with roux.

A general definition would simply be a thick, rich soup finished with cream.

Figure 136: Bisque

Cook the crustaceans

Add rice and seasonings

Add the highlighted crustaceans

—————— CLASSICAL SAUCES ——————

Classical sauces include the five "Mother Sauces," referred to as such because they constitute the base to hundreds of sauce recipes. The five Mother Sauces are Velouté, Béchamel, Tomato, Brown (also called Espagnole) and Hollandaise.

Velouté

As stated previously, this is a white stock thickened with a roux.

Figure 137: Creating a Velouté Sauce

Béchamel

A Béchamel is milk thickened with roux. Béchamel is used in many recipes of the Italian cuisine, e.g. Lasagne Emiliane.

Béchamel is used as the base for other sauces (such as Mornay sauce, which is Béchamel with cheese).

Figure 138: Add milk to roux

Figure 139: Cook until thick

Tomato Sauce

This sauce uses tomatoes that have been stewed with other flavorings and are then puréed until smooth. Usually served as part of a dish rather than as a condiment, Tomato sauces are common for meat and vegetables, but they are perhaps best known as sauces for pasta dishes.

Figure 140: Stew tomatoes

Figure 141: Purée to make sauce

Brown Sauce

In classical French cuisine, a brown sauce generally refers to a sauce with a meat stock base and reduced until thick. Today it is common for the roux to be left out and the sauce be naturally reduced to consistency. Brown sauce is also called "Espagnole" sauce and is used in the making of demi glace.

Hollandaise

Hollandaise belongs to a group that is based on an emulsion. It is a hot emulsified egg yolk sauce that is formed when melted butter (fat) is suspended into partially cooked egg yolks (water). Usually seasoned with lemon juice, salt, and a little white pepper or cayenne pepper, it is light yellow and opaque, smooth and creamy. The flavor is rich and buttery, with a mild tang from the citrus.

Figure 142: Start with eggs

Figure 143: Melt butter

Figure 144: Add lemon juice

Figure 145: Whip until thick

Demi Glace

Figure 146: Demi Glace

Literally translates to "half-glaze". This rich, highly flavored sauce is classically made by reducing equal parts of brown sauce and brown stock in half.

In today's contemporary kitchen the brown sauce is often eliminated and a straight reduction of brown veal stock is used to achieve a lighter version.

Considered a Classic Sauce, Demi Glace is _not_ considered a Mother Sauce, as it is created from a Brown Sauce.

CONTEMPORARY SAUCES

This grouping contains all the other sauces that are not based on the five mother sauces. Here are the most frequently seen examples.

Jus Lie

A thickened sauce made from stock. Commonly derived from the drippings left from a roast that are then mixed with stock and lightly tightened with a slurry.

A slurry is a mixture of cornstarch and liquid (usually water or stock) used to thicken a sauce or soup.

Figure 147: Creating a Jus Lie

Compound Butters

Flavored butters that are melted on top of meats and vegetables, used as a spread or used to finish various sauces.

A compound butter can be made by whipping additional elements, such as herbs, spices or aromatic liquids, into butter. The butter is then reformed, usually in plastic wrap or parchment paper, and chilled until it is firm enough to be sliced.

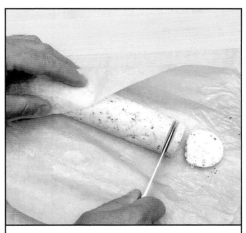

Figure 148: Compound butter

Gravy

A sauce derived from the rendered drippings of roasted meat. There are two basic types of meat gravy: thickened and unthickened. Unthickened gravy, in the case of red meats, is often referred to as "au jus." This is simply a cooked mixture of meat juices. Thickened gravies are usually made starting by adding flour or roux to the meat drippings in order to thicken the sauce.

Figure 149: Add roux to fat

Figure 150: Thickened Gravy

EMULSIONS

The following sauces are based on emulsions. An emulsion is created when fat is suspended in water. Emulsifying is done by slowly drizzling the fat into the liquid while mixing rapidly, resulting in a rich, satiny texture.

Beurre Blanc

A hot emulsion created by whipping softened butter into a reduction of shallots and wine.

Occasionally, heavy cream is added to provide stability to the "tempermental" sauce.

Figure 151: Creating a Beure Blanc

Vinaigrette

Figure 152: Vinaigrette

A basic oil and vinegar cold emulsion usually used to dress cold preparations.

Several garnishes may be added to spice up vinaigrette such as herbs, spices and shallots. Mustard is an emulsifier and adds flavor and stability when added to a vinaigrette.

Mayonnaise

A cold emulsion made of beaten raw egg yolk, oil, lemon juice or vinegar, and seasonings.

Homemade mayonnaise is a thick, creamy sauce, usually of a white or light yellow color. Commercial mayonnaise has lost some of the yellow color, due to the way they process egg yolks.

To reduce the danger of salmonella poisoning, commercial vendors pasteurize the yolks, or freeze them, and substitute water for most of their liquid, or use other emulsifiers in their mayonnaise.

Figure 153: Mayonnaise on the side

Rémoulade

Figure 154: Shrimp Rémoulade

Rémoulade is simply a mayonnaise that has mustard, capers, gherkins and herbs added to it.

Rémoulade sauce frequently accompanies seafood dishes such as pan-fried fish and salmon croquettes and is a classic condiment used in French and Cajun cooking.

Though traditional rémoulade is a creamy yellow shade, Louisiana-style rémoulade is usually red in color, thanks to the addition of ketchup, paprika, or cayenne pepper. Cajun rémoulade also includes other additions like parsley, green onions, and Worcestershire sauce, and the key ingredient in shrimp rémoulade.

MISCELLANEOUS SAUCES

Chutney

A chunky condiment of Indian origins made of chopped fruit, vinegar, sugar and spices.

Chutneys are presented as small dishes accompanying a meal and tend to be intensely seasoned.

Chutneys can be made fresh or cooked, and even preserved for long-term storage.

These little dishes are used to brighten and offset larger amounts of starchy food such as rice and highlight the flavors of meats and breads.

Figure 155: Assorted Chutneys

Compote

Figure 156: Compote Dessert

Compote is a fine puree of cooked fruit made usually with a base of apple, with the possible addition of apricot, pear or various other fruits, which can then be used as a base for other desserts.

Compote may also be a dessert containing diced fresh or dried fruits that have been cooked in flavorful syrup.

Whole fruits are immersed in water and with sugar and spices added to the dish, and cooked over gentle heat.

Salsa

Spanish for "sauce." It usually is a spicy, uncooked preparation of vegetables or fruit, especially tomatoes, onions, and chili peppers.

While often used in Mexican cuisine, salsa's use is expanding as it can include a wide range of ingredients including black beans, tomato, corn, tomatilla, mango, watermelon, peach, strawberry, and more.

Often served with fried totilla chips, salsa is also used as either a complement or sause over other items, including tacos.

Figure 157: Salsa and Chips

Coulis

Figure 158: Coulis

A thick sauce that is a purée of a fruit or vegetables.

A vegetable coulis is commonly used on meat and vegetable dishes, and it can also be used as a base for soups or other sauces.

Fruit coulis are most often used on desserts. Raspberry coulis, for example, is especially popular with poached apples.

Garde Manger

Garde manger, meaning "keep to eat" refers to an cold pantry area where cold dishes (such as salads, hors d'œuvres, appetizers, canapes, pates and terrines) are prepared and other foods are stored under refrigeration.

Forcemeat

Figure 159: Forcemeat

Forcemeat is a mixture of ground meat or seafood and other ingredients used for sausages, pâté and other preparations.

Galantine

A forcemeat (usually poultry) that is rolled and poached in its own skin.

Aspic

A clear jelly made from a flavorful liquid that has been thickened with gelatin. May be used to coat food or cubed and served as a garnish.

Canapé

A hors d'oeuvre consisting of a small piece of toast to which a garnish is mounted upon.

Canapés can be either hot or cold.

Figure 160: Canapé variety

Gravlax

A Scandinavian dish of raw salmon cured with salt, sugar and dill.

Figure 161: Gravlax

Timbale

A small bucket-shaped mold used to shape custards, mousselines and other items. It is also a preparation made in such a mold.

Mousse

A light, foamy dish made by folding whipped egg whites and/or whipped cream into a flavorful base.

A mousse can be either hot or cold.

Figure 162: Mousse

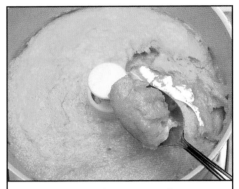

Figure 163: Mousseline

Mousseline

A forcemeat that has been lightened with cream and eggs.

Figure 164: Quenelle

Quenelle

A light, poached dumpling of mousseline that has been formed into the shape of an egg.

Figure 165: Pâté en Croûte

Pâté en Croûte

Pâté, which is a mixture of ground meat and fat minced into a spreadable past, baked in a pastry crust.

Sausage

A forcemeat that has been pumped into a natural or artificial casing.

Figure 166: Sausage

Cured Meat

A item that has been preserved by means of salting, smoking or dehydration.

Figure 167: Cured Meat

Terrine / Pâté

Forcemeat of meat and/or vegetables, baked in a mold.

Figure 168: Pâté

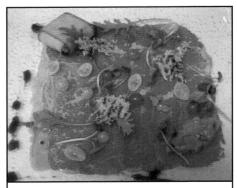

Figure 169: Carpaccio

Carpaccio

Classically, an Italian dish consisting of very thin slices of raw beef served with vinaigrette. Today, the term carpaccio can also be used for thinly pounded fish.

Figure 170: Tartare

Tartare

Traditionally, Tartare is minced beef served raw with an egg yolk and seasonings.

Today, chefs are making Tartare with ingredients such as salmon and tuna.

Figure 171: Ceviché

Ceviché

Small pieces of fish that are "cooked" by means of an acid, usually from citrus fruits.

Baking and Pastry Terms

Bavarian Cream

A delicate cream that is stiffened with gelatin, mixed with whipped cream and fruit purée or other flavorings, and then set in a mold.

Pastry Cream

Also called by its French name "Crème Patissière."

This thick egg custard is used for the production of Napoleons, éclairs, cream puffs, soufflés, cakes and tarts

Mousse

A light soft dessert that is similar to a Bavarian cream, but usually does not contain gelatin. A mousse may be piped into a container, but will not set in a mold.

Figure 172: Napoleon Dessert

Pâté a Choux

Dough created by combining flour with boiling water and butter. Eggs are then beaten in to achieve a smooth paste.

When baked, the eggs make the pastry expand, creating a delicate shell with a hollow center. Cream puffs, profiteroles and éclairs are common pâté-a-choux specialties.

Tuile

Classically is a thin, crisp almond cookie that resembles a curved tile. Today, a Tuile is made in many different shapes and is flavored with ingredients other than almonds.

Petit Four

Figure 173: Petit Four

Sometimes known as Mignardises, these bite-sized confections are served either with or after the main dessert.

Puff Pastry

Figure 174: Apple Turnover

A rich and delicate pastry made up of very thin layers. The dough is rolled and folded in such a way that several layers of butter and dough are created.

When baked, the moisture in the butter turns to steam, causing the dough to puff and separate into a flaky pastry.

Puff Pastry has no added leavener, when yeast is added to this dough it is then croissant or Danish dough. Napoleons, turnovers and Vol-au-Vents are made from puff dough.

Phyllo Dough

Phyllo literally comes from the Greek word for leaf. It is lean dough that is kneaded and stretched to a single tissue thin layer.

Phyllo and strudel doughs are very similar.

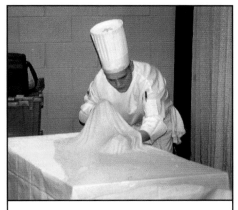

Figure 175: Chef Lon Symensma pulling Phyllo

Sherbet

A frozen mixture similar to sorbet but in which, while remaining low fat and with a granular/Icy texture, cream or milk have been added.

Sorbet

A frozen mixture, water based, that is softer and more granular than ice cream. Flavors are usually fruit or herb based. Because it does not contain any fat or egg yolk, it is common to serve a very lightly sweetened sorbet before the entree course as a palate cleanser.

Figure 176: Sorbet Flavors

Restrictive Diets

Restaurants attract many types of clientele. Some individuals have specific dietary needs and other have special dietary requests. Usually if dietary needs are a priority for the customer, he or she will announce or inquire about specific menu items, ingredients, and let the establishment know about any special restrictions. Even though it is ultimately up to the chef to provide a nourishing meal that meets the customers' needs, it is the service staff that must communicate the needs of the customer to the chef. Therefore, it is important to understand the different types of diets. Servers help make the customers feel confident that their specific needs are going to be understood and met. This section discusses the major dietary restrictions a dining room professional will likely encounter.

VEGETARIAN

One of the most common dietary preferences is Vegetarianism. In general, vegetarians eat a diet that is rich in fruit and vegetables as well as nuts and other plant-based or non-animal foods.

Figure 177: Honey

Vegetarians refrain from eating products derived from animal processing such as gelatin, which is derived from the collagen found in an animal's skin and bones. Most vegetarians will, however, eat food produced by animals such as milk, cheese, eggs and honey.

People generally practice vegetarianism out of ethical or religions beliefs while others may adopt a vegetarian diet as a means of being more health conscious. There are a number of factors that may inspire an individual to become vegetarian that may include concerns regarding the humane treatment of animals or environmental sustainability.

There are a number of sub-categories of vegetarianism, each of which defines a vegetarian's level of tolerance in regards to what they may or may not include in their diet. As a professional in the dining room, it is important to understand these differences and communicate effectively with your guests when discussing various menu options.

Semi-vegetarians

Semi vegetarians include small amounts of fish and/or chicken in their diet.

Figure 178: Semi-vegetarian chart

Raw foodists

Raw foodists eat only uncooked non-meat foods.

Figure 179: Raw foodists chart

Lacto-ovo vegetarians

Lacto-ovo vegetarians eat eggs and dairy, but no meat.

Figure 180: Lacto-ovo vegetarian chart

Lacto vegetarians

Lacto vegetarians consume dairy products, but no meat or eggs.

Figure 181: Lacto vegetarian chart

Ovo vegetarians

Ovo vegetarians eat eggs, but no dairy products or meat.

Figure 182: Ovo vegetarians chart

Vegans

Vegans eat no meat, dairy products, or eggs.

Figure 183: Vegan chart

Macrobiotic vegetarians

Macrobiotic vegetarians live on whole grains, sea and land vegetables, beans and miso.

Figure 184: Macrobiotic chart

Fruitarians

Fruitarians consume fruits, nuts, and seeds, and certain vegetables.

Figure 185: Fruitarians chart

Natural hygienists

Natural hygienists eat plant foods and combine foods in certain ways. They also believe in a periodic fasting.

Figure 186: Natural hygienists chart

Noninterventionist vegetarians

Noninterventionist vegetarians are Fruitarians who take no living things for food, but rely on fallen nuts, fruits, and vegetables, and on seeds that can be harvested without killing the host plant.

Figure 187: Noninterventionist chart

MACROBIOTIC

The word Macrobiotic is from the Greek word Makro (great) and Bios (life) and it means "the great way of life." It is based on the ancient Chinese concept of Yin and Yang.

Figure 188: Yin and Yang

Yang consists of fire, pressure, salt, and time (aging). Yin is oil, water, lack of pressure, and freshness. Yin and Yang are not absolute, but a matter of degree. The ultimate goal of a macrobiotic diet is to avoid extremes of either Yin or Yang.

All foods fall into a spectrum of Yin and Yang. Examples of Yin foods are tropical fruits, refined grains, milk, butter, concentrated sweeteners, maple syrup, honey, refined sugar, alcohol, spices, chemical additives, drugs, and medications.

Examples of Yang foods include salt, egg, meat, poultry, hard salty cheese, fish, and seafood. Brown rice is considered the food item in the middle of the spectrum and is very important in the macrobiotic menu.

Macrobiotics is not a fixed regime; it is based on flexible adaptation to the constant changing environment.

Here is a summary of the principles:
1. Eat according to tradition-tracing whole grains and vegetables to the origins of our species.

2. Vary diet according to climate-not eating foods that are imported from another climate.

3. Vary diet according to season, emphasizing Yang foods and cooking techniques in the cold winter months and serving more Yin, fresh, lightly cooked food, during the summer.

4. Vary diet according to personal need.

HINDUISM

Hinduism is a vast complex of beliefs that is concentrated in India. One of the most important concepts at the root of Hinduism is the idea of sacrifice. Grains are offered to the gods before being eaten, for example, and whatever is left behind is considered pure for the spirit. Hindus generally eat two times a day, after the morning and evening prayers. The sacred text puts importance on the idea that man is what he eats. Thus, the way food is prepared and when it is eaten in is important.

Figure 189: Grains

KOSHER

A Kosher diet is one that adheres to the laws of Kashrut. Foods that are Kosher are permitted and foods that are Terefah are forbidden.

For a meal to be Kosher the milk and meat must be separated and the slaughter and preparation of meat must be carried out in a specific manner. There are also restrictions as to meat and fish types. Animals that are herbivores and have cloven hooves are considered clean and are permitted.

Figure 190: Kosher Sympols

They must only eat grass and plants, the cloven hooves ensure that they cannot hold prey and are not carnivores.

All other animals such as pig, rabbit, horse, and beasts of prey are forbidden. All birds of prey and certain birds such as owls, storks, and ostriches are not permitted.

Figure 191: Separate milk & meat

Furthermore, any animal that has died of natural causes or of disease may not be consumed. Nor can game that has been hunted and killed by gunshot be eaten. An animal must be killed in a Kosher way for the animal to be considered Kosher, and there is no way to make an animal Kosher if it is not Kosher from the beginning.

From the sea, only fish that have both fins and scales are permitted. Certain fish are forbidden such as sturgeon, swordfish, monkfish, ray, rockfish, skate, turbot, shark, eel, shellfish, crustaceans, sea urchins, octopus, squid, reptiles, turtles, frog, snake, and insects.

All fish does not need to be killed in the ritualistic manner, but flesh from bone cannot be separated on the Sabbath.

MUSLIM

The Muslim diet is structured by dietary laws set out in the Qur'an and Hadith. There are three categories of food.

The first is halal that is lawful. The second is haram, which is prohibited. The third is makruh that is considered reprehensible, but which is not subject to the same degree of prohibition as haram. Alcohol, split brood, pork, dogs, excrement, carrion and the milk of animals whose flesh is not eaten is forbidden.

There is a complex body of laws which state which foods are allowed, which foods are forbidden, and when there are exceptions. Like Kosher law, slaughter is subject to religious law and rules concerning hunting wild animals vary. Likewise, a slaughter must involve a clean cut to the throat to be considered halal. This ensures that the aorta is cut and all of the blood drains from the meat completely.

BUDDHISM

Buddhism began in India in the 6th Century BC, but it is also considered a main religion in Sri Lanka, Burma, Thailand, Laos, Japan, and Cambodia.

Buddhists believe in reincarnation and that the soul of the human will at one time inhabit an animal. Thus, Buddhists do not believe in killing or injuring any living creatures. This would indicate that they are vegetarians, but many Buddhists do eat meat.

They believe that the real wrong doing would be in killing a living animal so, in many cases, the animal may have just died, may have been killed by a non-Buddhist,

Figure 192: Buddhist Temple

or may have been in an accident. Buddhist practices are flexible for example; it is permitted to eat meat for the sake of one's survival.

Also, it would be considered better to take the life of a large animal over that of a small animal because a larger animal would produce more meat.

Figure 193: Vegetable Assortment

—————— CHRISTIAN ——————

Christianity is one of the major religions of the world and generally has no taboos, which would forbid believers to eliminate or avoid certain foods. One particular issue to note is that Christians feast and fast. Christmas and Easter are two examples of feasting and Lent is an example of fasting. Christmas involves a main meal on Christmas Eve or Christmas Day to celebrate the birth of Christ. Either occasion is one for which a family will get together and share a special meal. There are many popular dishes, which are served and they vary from country to country.

Figure 194: Christians praying

Figure 195: Easter

Easter celebrates the day that Jesus rose from the dead and it also marks the end of the fasting period of Lent. There are special foods that are associated with Easter such as eggs and lamb.

Eggs signify the rebirth and lamb is symbolic because Jesus is considered the Lamb of God. Lent is the period of forty (40) days from Ash Wednesday to Easter Eve. It is a period of fasting and specific details vary with the different churches.

Christians are supposed to eat fish only on Fridays and abstain from eating meat, particularly during the fasting season of Lent.

This is reflected in the fact that in many restaurants, especially in Europe, are conscious of having a 'fish special' on their Friday menu, even if fish is not the primary focus of the restaurant.

Allergies

When a customer lets a server know that they are allergic to a certain food, the meal preparation needs special consideration. Understanding the basic food allergies will help to ensure that diners have a safe dining experience. Common allergies include milk, wheat, corn, eggs, shellfish, fish, soy foods, peanuts, and other nuts. There are also special elimination diets that include gluten-free and yeast-free.

After eating a food containing a protein to which one is allergic, the immune system releases antibodies. Common reactions to allergens include loss of consciousness, wheezing, hoarseness, shortness of breath, difficulty swallowing, swelling of the face, eyelids, lips, hands, and feet, hives and itching around the mouth, face, hands, scalp, and feet. Avoiding the common allergens can be difficult. This section will help you to avoid foods with allergens.

WHEAT-FREE

Wheat is a cereal grain that is harvested and used to produce four and semolina. Semolina is ground wheat that is ground more coursely than flour and resembles cornmeal in appearance.

For allergies to wheat, the most obvious foods to avoid are breads, bagels, matzo buns, pita, breaded foods, stuffing, pizza, croutons, bulgar (tabouli), couscous, crackers, cornbread, dumplings, muffins, pancakes, pastas, piecrusts, pretzels, waffles, and most cookies.

In package foods, one must avoid flour, semolina, graham, durum, vial wheat gluten, gluten, wheat starch, cracked wheat, farina, and bran. Other not so obvious food sources that contain wheat are barley malt, chocolate, cocoa, MSG, soy sauce, tamari, and some alcoholic beverages (most notably wheat beer).

Figure 196: Foods to Avoid for persons with Wheat Allergies

DAIRY-FREE

To avoid dairy, one must avoid milk and milk byproducts. This includes whey, casein, caseinate, lactose, lactate, lactoalbumin, and lacto-globulin. Cream, milk, butter, and cheese are forms of dairy one must avoid, but can be commonly found in cakes, cookies, breads, batters, puddings, gravies, sauces, and some soups. Salad dressings should also be checked and sausages sometimes contain dry milk.

Figure 197: Foods to Avoid for persons with Dairy Allergies

CORN-FREE

If one is allergic to corn, it is obvious that corn on the cob must be avoided, but what must also be avoided is corn sweeteners, corn oil, cornstarch, and cornmeal. There are many prepared foods which contain corn, one must check labels to be sure. Most sour things contain corn.

For example, most vinegar used in commercial products is distilled from corn. Pickles, salad dressings, mustard, mayonnaise, relish, and sauerkraut must be verified.

Other foods or ingredients that contain corn are cheeses, vanilla, xantham gum, MSG, monoglycerides, diglycerides, and gelatin.

Figure 198: White Vinegar

EGG-FREE

Eggs are used to make a number of products.

The following is a list of foods which contain eggs or egg product: ice cream, sherbet, meatballs, meatloaf, macaroons, cream pies, frosting, mayonnaise, tartar sauce, some baked products, and quick breads.

Figure 199: Ice Cream and Meatballs

YEAST-FREE

Avoiding yeast does not simply mean avoiding baked goods that use bakers yeast as a leavener. The following is a list of what a typical yeast-free diet avoids: Barley malt, maltodextrin, vinegar, chocolate, pickles, pickled food, alcoholic beverages, non-alcoholic beer, aged cheeses, soy sauce, Worcestershire, cottonseed oil, nuts, peanuts, apples, grapes, coffee, hot dogs, salami, bacon, processed meats containing nitrates or nitrites.

This is a basic list of foods, but a common rule to remember is to avoid fermented foods and to stick with fresh food. To substitute for vinegar, one can use lemon juice and fresh cheeses such as mozzarella can be used to replace aged cheeses.

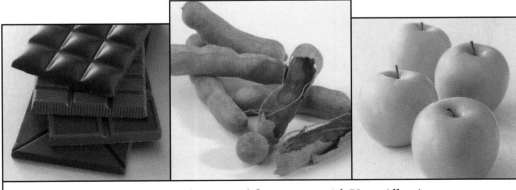

Figure 200: Foods to Avoid for persons with Yeast Allergies

GLUTEN-FREE

A gluten-free diet is similar to a wheat-free diet, but also avoid grains related to wheat, that is rye, oats, and barley.

Gluten is a part of wheat that triggers allergic reactions and what is known as Celiac Disease. Some glutens hide under different names on labels.

The following is a list of what to avoid:

- Hydrolyzed vegetable protein.
- Vinegar distilled from a wheat or wheat related grain.
- Flavorings or extracts that use a forbidden grain.
- Caramel color made with malt syrup.
- Dextrin can be made with wheat.
- Triticale which is a cereal grain that is a cross of wheat and rye.
- Rice syrup.
- Sirimi which is imitation seafood created with a starch binder.
- Candy may be wheat free, but when it is packaged, it is put on the conveyor belt with flour.
- Instant powdered coffee, decaffeinated coffee, and tea.

Figure 201: Foods to Avoid for persons with Gluten Allergies

Figure 202: Foods to Avoid for persons with Allergies

3 | Beer & Cocktails

This section contains information on:

- Beer Essentials.

- Beer Service.

- Cocktail Essentials.

SECTION THREE

Beer & Cocktails

Objectives

By the end of this section, you should be able to...

- List and explain four (4) ingredients to make beer.

- List nine steps (9) to make beer.

- Explain the difference between the two categories of beer.

- Perform beer service in a pilsner glass.

- List the four components of a cocktail order.

- List and explain the most common cocktail mixing methods.

Beer & Cocktail Essentials

Beer Essentials

Beer is recorded as one of the oldest beverages humans have produced, dating back as far back as the 5th millennium BC in records of Ancient Egypt and Mesopotamia! Today, beer is still enjoyed by countless billions around the world.

──────────────── BEER INGREDIENTS ────────────────

Generally speaking, beer is a bitter-tasting alcoholic drink brewed by fermenting malt and yeast, and then flavoring it with hops. **Beer is made from four very basic ingredients:**

1. Water.
2. Fermentable Sugar (Malted Barley).
3. Hops.
4. Yeast.

Water

Water used to make beer need only to be drinkable and low in chlorine levels. This is the largest ingredient, by volume, of all the ingredients. Some commercial breweries chemically treat the water used in the brewing process to make sure this key ingredient is the same for every brewing, with a desired "hardness" and pH.

Fermentable Sugar (Malted Barley)

The fermentable sugar used to make beer is made from malted barley. Barley is a cereal plant with a long head of whiskered grains (Figure 203) that has many uses, one of which happens to be the production of malt. Rice, corn, and pure sugar are sometimes used as a less expensive substitute, but those options add little to the overall flavor. Malt is the backbone of beer because it creates a strong, sweet flavor.

It is malt that determines the beer's overall body (the way the beer feels in your mouth) and final color / flavor.

Figure 203: Barley

Hops

Hops come from a climbing vine of the mulberry family. Its green, female flowers look like little pinecones. It is these flowers that are then dried and used in the brewing process to add a distinctive bitter taste to the beer.

Hops also act as a preservative by lowering the amount of bacteria that can grow in beer.

Hops are what give the beer its "head", or foam, at the top of the glass.

Figure 204: Hops

Yeast

Yeast is a single-celled living organism that lives its whole life cycle during the beer making process. *Yeast feeds off of the sugars in the malt.* As it feeds, the yeast creates alcohol and carbon dioxide, and gives the beer its flavor and carbonation.

Yeast is the final factor of the style and flavor of the beer. Although there are many hundreds of different types of yeast, they can be divided into two separate categories:

1. Ale yeast.
2. Lager yeast.

The Brewmaster determines what type of yeast to use depending on the style of beer that is being brewed.

Without yeast, the mix of ingredients would not ferment, and beer would not be created!

Figure 205: Making Beer

--- BREWING STEPS ---

The process of brewing beer is an age-old technique changing very little over the course of time. Generally speaking, **all beer is created by using the following nine steps:**

1. Grain is milled into a fine powder.
2. Hot water is added to the 'cracked' malt, creating 'wort'.
3. Bring the wort to a boil.
4. Boil, or brew, the wort mix up to two hours, slowly adding the desired amount of hops.
5. Cool the mixture and add yeast.
6. Move the cooled wort to the first holding tank, where the yeast converts the sugar (maltose) to alcohol.
7. Move the mix to a second tank where sugar is added, which re-energizes the yeast. The yeast consumes the sugar and creates bubbles in the process (carbon dioxide - CO_2).
8. Bottle the beer, trapping the CO_2.
9. Heat the bottles, called pasteurization.

--- TYPES OF BEER ---

Beers can be broken down into two major categories:

1. Ales.

2. Lagers.

The difference between these two groups is in how they are brewed and the type of yeast used in the brewing process.

There are literally thousands of different strains of yeast available to the brewer and each will give off its own unique flavor to the finished product.

Ales and lagers can be further broken down into many sub-categories and styles.

Figure 206: Oktoberfest in Germany

Ales

Generally, ales are rich in character and dark in color. Ales use top-fermenting yeasts at warmer temperatures between 55 and 75 degrees Fahrenheit.

The time to produce ale beer is usually short. The major categories of ales include Stouts, Wheat beer, Trappist/Abbey ales, Brown ales, Pale ales, Saison and Porters.

Stouts

Stouts are generally made from pale or caramel malts and roasted un-malted barley. Typical stouts are known for their very dark black color, creamy white head, and rich flavor. Generally, stouts tend to have a heavy barley character and a low hop rate. Beers in this category span a taste range from sweetness to bitterness.

Examples: Guinness® and Irish "Dry" Stouts

Figure 207: Guiness Stout

Wheat beer

Wheat beers use a high proportion of malted wheat to create a fuller bodied, highly effervescent, low-alcohol beer. They generally have a cloudy, bright yellow appearance and smell of vanilla, clove and often banana.
Examples: Hefeweizen ('hefe' is German for yeast) and Weissbire, or "white beer"

Trappist / Abbey ales

In order to be truly labeled Trappist, these beers must be brewed in one of six Belguim brewing monasteries; otherwise they are referred to as Abbey Ales. *This style of ale is commonly dark amber in color, full-bodied, moderate to high in alcohol, and have a special bottle, which results in yeasty sediments.*

Brown ales

Brown ales are generally brown in color, slightly sweet and have lightly hopped features. Some brown ales, such as the Newcastle Brown, are somewhat nutty in taste. This character is because roasted caramel malt is used during brewing.
<u>Examples:</u> Winter, Scottish, Irish, and cream ales

Pale ales

Pale ales are typically amber or copper in color, drawing from the use of pale malts and tend to be slightly dry and bitter.
<u>Example:</u> India Pale Ale or I.P.A.

Saison

Saison beers tend to be light in color and body. They are brewed slightly higher in alcohol, and have a typical fruity sourness.

Porter

Generally medium-bodied and dark in color, porters vary in alcohol content, bitterness, and hop rate, but lack the bite of roasted barley found in their cousin, the stout.

British Ales	*German Ale*
Bitter	Altbier
Mild	Kölsh
Pale Ale	*American Cream Ale*
Brown Ale	*Belgian Specialty Ale*
Stout	Saison
Barley Wine	White Beer
Porter	Trappist Ale
Scottish Ale	
Wheat Beers	
Weizenbier	
Unkelweizen	
Belgian Lambic	
American Wheat Beer	

Figure 208: Ale Beer Examples

Lagers

Typical lagers are light in body and color, and have a crisp taste. Lagers use bottom-fermenting yeasts at cooler temperatures between 32 and 55 degrees Fahrenheit.

The process to produce lager beer can be long. Because of the cooler temperature that lagers ferment, they are less likely to grow bacteria during the fermentation step.

The major categories of ales include Pilsner, German bock / Dopplebock, Oktoberfest, Vienna-style lagers, American / Australian lagers, and California Common / Steam Beer.

Pilsner

Pilsners are generally pale golden in color, and light and crisp to the taste. Czech pilsners present a richly sweet malt-laden brew with a lots of bubbles.

German pilsners, 'Pils' for short, tend to be more bitter than the Czech types. *Pilsners often have spicy, floral flavors and smells. They also have a thick, rich head of foam.*

Figure 209: Pilsner Beer

German bock / Dopplebock

These beers can be brewed either dark or light (helles) in color and range between 6 and 14 percent alcohol. German bocks are brewed to bring out the sweetness of the malt. Very little hops are used in this style. The goal is to use just enough to complement the rich malt flavor.

Oktoberfest

Oktoberfest beers are amber-orange in color. These highly malty brews are balanced by a noticable hop bitterness. Like it's counterpart Märzen (German for March), Oktoberfest beers are traditionally brewed in October in preparation for the fall festival.

Vienna-style

This beer type is similar to the beers of Oktoberfest with a red-amber to copper color, but have a much milder malt characteristic.
<u>Example:</u> Negra Modelo

American / Australian lagers

By adding corn and rice to the brewing, these lagers are lighter than their closest relative, the Pilsner. American lager, also know as the American Standard variety of beer, is usually brewed with a mild hop amount. *This type of beer is the most popular in North America.*
<u>Example:</u> Budweiser, Coors, Molson, Fosters

California Common / Steam Beer

This type of beer is brewed at ale fermenting temperatures while using a special type of lager yeast. Brewed nearly exclusively by the Anchor Brewing Company in San Francisco, California, this beer typically has a malty sweetness because it uses caramel or crystal malt.

German &
    Continental Lagers
 Pilsner
 Oktoberfest
 Märzen
 Vienna Lager
 Bock/Doppelbock
 Munich Helles
 Dunkel
 Australian Lagers
	American Lagers
	 American Standard
	 American Premium
	 Dry Beer
	 California Common
	    Beer
	 American Dark Beers

Figure 210: Lager Beer Examples

Beer Service

For nearly every type of beer brewed there is a glass that is considered appropriate for its service. In Belgium, it is actually common to have a beer that has been designed around the shape of the glass!

Just as the shape of a wine glass can be matched with different wines, so can the glass a beer is served in. *Why?*

Because the shape of the beer glass can impact the way a beer is enjoyed. The way a glass is shaped, along with the way the beer is poured into it, can change the amount of foam, or "head", that is created on top of the beer and also allows more of the unique flavors to be released.

BEER GLASSWARE

Generally speaking, the two most popular types of glasses are:

1. **Pilsner.**
2. **Pint.**

Pilsner Glass

This 12-ounce glass is used with a variety of light beer styles.

Originally designed to show off German lager beers, this tall, slender glass has a wide mouth that tapers downward to a small pedestal or short-stemmed bottom.

The shape of this glass helps release the bubbles in the beer.

Figure 211: Pilsner Glass

Pint Glass

Figure 212: Pint Glass

This Tumbler style of glass is probably the most common glass used to serve beer in the United States.

Even though there are variations, the pint glass usually comes in two distinct sizes:

1. 16-ounce US Tumbler.
2. 20-ounce Imperial or Nonic.

The shape of this glass is generally round, but the 20-ounce style has a bump near the top that makes it easy to hold and easy to stack.

Remember that when handling glassware, the rules of sanitation come first!

Besides keeping your hands and beer glasses clean, know that left-over soap from washing can also change the taste and presentation of beer.

Usually, it is best to hand-wash beer glasses. If a film is still on the glasses after washing, they may need to be polished.

Even though it is fairly common to serve a cold glass with beer, if there is too much condensation on the inside of the glass, the beer's flavor might be diluted.

Be sure to know how your customer wants to enjoy his beer and offer him a choice of glassware!

Other Glassware

Available in many sizes, the Bavarian Weizen glass is specifically designed to promote and capture the rich creamy head found on wheat beers such as the Hefeweizen.

Like the pilsner glass, its shape helps to accentuate these highly carbonated brews while highlighting their hazy golden color. Their wide mouth is more spherical and it's thin walls taper slowly to rest on a thick knobby base.

Beer steins are highly decorated, mug-like, vessels that are typically reserved for festive occasions or decoration.

Figure 213: Bavarian Beer Stein

The Mug is another favorite design that can accommodate a larger volume of beer. Sturdily made of thick, heavy glass or porcelain with a handle, which allows for a better grip when toasting with a vigorous "clink".

A similar design, the stein, was invented in the era of the black plague with a hinged metal lid and thumb-lift that discouraged diseased flies from dropping in. Although it's dimpled exterior or decorative coating hides the beer's appearance, this mug makes for an nice way to enjoy a celebratory brew.

Figure 214: Mug Glass

Figure 215: Tulip Glass

Other more specialty vessels, such as goblets, tulips and snifters can be used to promote aeration through swirling and the release of delicate volatiles found in strong Scottish ales or Belgian Trappist beers.

Tulips are specifically designed to induce and support large, foamy heads. Seated on a short stem, their large bulbous bottoms close to a tight, narrow opening. This allows for the faintest of aromas to be channeled directly to the nose of the taster.

Snifter type glasses, even though they discourage head retention, soften the harsh alcoholic overtones of strong ales, and allow the taster to pleasantly swirl the beer as you would the finest brandy. Likewise a goblet or oversized wine glass

would achieve the same end result, allowing for ample headspace while drawing attention to the nose of the beer.

Keep in mind that proper handling procedures apply to beer glasses, too. Residue from machine washes may inhibit head retention and even alter the taste of some beers. Hand washing is recommended. If a machine with chemical rinse and sanitation cycles is used, however, polishing may be required to limit residue.

Glasses may be chilled prior to presentation; however the condensation this creates on the inside of the glass may dilute the beers flavor and even alter the serving temperature of specialty beers. Be conscious of your guests' appreciation for the beverage and offer choice glassware.

Figure 216: Hold glass by its bottom half

POURING BEER

With so many different types and styles of beer -- and as just as many different glasses to pour them in -- there are a few different ways to get the beer from the bottle into the glass.

A number of customers like to pour their beer themselves. So when thinking about whether or not to pour the beer for a guest, it is best to ask them before you start!

To pour a beer into a Pilsner glass, follow this simple two-step process:

1. ***Bring a glass***, usually chilled, and the beer to the table.
2. ***Pour the beer*** gently against the inside of the glass. *Two ways to do this are:*

   a. Grab the rim of the glass with the lip of the bottle. Lean the glass over slightly tipping it gently (holding it stable with the lip of the bottle) and tilt the beer bottle's bottom up slowly so that beer flows smoothly against the inside of the glass (Figure 217). This option requires you pay close attention to how much the glass is tipped over.
   No customer wants to get wet!

   b. Don't touch the glass with the bottle, but pour the beer gently on the inside of the glass (Figure 218). This is easier to do if you pick up the glass and tilt it slightly, but it can be done by leaving the glass on the table.

For a Pint glass, simly pour the last bit of the beer directly in the center of the glass.

The result is a perfect amount of foam (aim for about 1/4 inch) that floats on top of the beer!

Figure 217: Place the bottle on the rim

Figure 218: Pour beer against the side

Cocktail Essentials

The art of making a cocktail drink is called "mixology".

There are many books published about mixology and there are literally thousands of cocktails. Even though each bar could make slight changes to a cocktail, the basic principles of mixology remain fairly standard.

───────── FOUR COMPONENTS OF AN ORDER ─────────

The making of almost every type of cocktail includes at least three out of the four following components:

> *1. Alcohol.*
> *2. Method.*
> *3. Serving (Mixing and Style).*
> *4. Garnish.*

Remember these four components and you can make sure you can explain to a bartender what the guest wants, even if you don't know how the cocktail is made!

Alcohol

Gather the following two pieces of information for the alcohol portion of the order:

1. <u>What category of alcohol should be used?</u>
   Many cocktails were created by using a specific kind of liquor. For example, the Martini originally was created with a base of Gin. Over time, many people replaced Vodka for Gin. *To be safe, check what type of alcohol a guest wants in the drink.*

2. <u>What brand of alcohol should be used?</u>
   Different brands (for the same type of liquor) really do taste different! But besides that, many people order a specific brand name as a status statement. Usually, when a guest wants a specific brand of alcohol, they normally mention it first. For example, a guest ordering a "Manhattan" (which main liquor is supposed to be whiskey) may ask for a "CC Manhattan". That signals that the drink is to be made with Canadian Club® whiskey.

All alcohol brands are divided into four categories, each generally matched to a price range. These categories are generally named:

1. *House Brands.*
2. *Call Brands.*
3. *Premium Brands.*
4. *Top Shelf (Super Premium Brands).*

Which brands are put into each category can change from one restaurant to the next.

So it is important to know the way each establishment categorizes its liquors. Understanding these categories and the difference prices can benefit the guest, the server and the restuarant.

Method

Method means two things:

1. *The way a cocktail is mixed, and*
2. *What is its texture.*

The cocktail method is to a bartender what a cooking recipe is for a chef. The method is made up of ingredients *plus* the way the ingredients are mixed together. *Here are a couple examples of very well known methods:*

1. A Martini is 11/2 ounces of Gin and 1/2 ounces of dry Vermouth stirred with ice, but it can be asked for in the following ways:
   a. Extra Dry: 13/4 ounces of Gin and 1/4 ounce of dry Vermouth.
   b. Dry: 12/3 ounces of Gin and 1/3 ounce of dry Vermouth.
   c. Sweet: 11/2 ounce of Gin, 3/4 ounce of sweet Vermouth.
   d. Dirty: Add some of the olive juice to the mix.

2. Making a drink "Sour", which is adding the juice of half a lemon and half a teaspoon of powdered sugar. Today, Sour mixes are often pre-made for the bartender. Examples of liquor used with Sour are: Whiskey Sour, Gin Sour and Vodka Sour.

Mixing and Style

There technically two pieces to the 'Serving' part of a coctail order: Mixing and Style.

Mixing

A cocktail order can include, even though it is rare, the description of the mixing method. Who will ever forget the famous line by the English spy, *007*, "Shaken, not stirred."

The most common mixing styles are:

> *1) Shaken,*   *2) Bruised, and*   *3) Stirred.*

Shaken

Shaken utilizes a shaker (Figure 219) that is partially filled with rock ice (Figure 220) plus the cocktail's ingredients. Utilizing a shaker (Figure 221) not only cools the mix, but also melts some of the ice into the mix, which slightly lightens the taste of the drink.

Figure 219: A Shaker

Figure 220: Adding ice

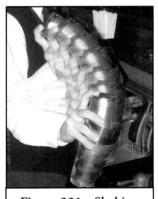

Figure 221: Shaking

Bruised

Signifies that the ingredients are placed in a shaker and shaken harder and longer than normal. The result is that some of the ice is reduced to small flakes that resemble 'bruises,' named because they appear clear, but are still solid.

Stirred

When a drink is order 'Stirred', the bartender is being instructed by the customer to not shake the cocktail.

This means that the bartender must use a type of mixing spoon to gently stir the cocktail.

A type of spoon is shown in Figure 222.

Figure 222: Stirring Spoon Example

The result is that the cocktail still gets chilled, just not as violently as when it is shaken, which means that less of the ice melts into the drink.

Customers who don't want to dilute their drink sometimes order their cocktail 'stirred'.

Style

Most cocktails use ice as a step in their preparation. *Whether or not the ice is kept in with the mix depends on the style of serving.* **The style that a cocktail is served dictates the way the cocktail is presented to the guest. The style impacts:**

- *The type of glass used.*
- *The amount of ice in the mix.*
- *The texture.*

There are typically five main cocktail service styles:

1. On the Rocks.
2. Tall.
3. Up.
4. Neat.
5. Frozen.

On The Rocks

The style means that a cocktail is served in some type of Rock glass filled with ice.

There are several ways a cocktail can be prepared "on the rocks." The easiest way is to put the ice into a glass and pour the alcohol on top, as shown below.

Figure 223: Creating an "On the Rocks" cocktail

Another alternative is to use the shaken method and then pour all the ingredients, including the ice, into a Rock glass.

A bartender may choose to strain the ice out from within the shaker so that the drink can be poured over fresh ice, as shown in Figure 224.

Figure 224: Alternative way to create an "On the Rocks" cocktail

Tall

Tall is a serving that generally applies to mixtures that include a soft drink (such as club soda, Sprite®, Coke®, or even milk) and are served over ice.

A tall glass allows the bartender to vary the amount of the non-alcoholic mix to be added. That way, the bartender can change how strong a drink he makes.

Figure 225: Creating a "Tall" cocktail

Here is how to make a tall drink:
1. *Fill a glass with ice.*
2. *Pour the alcohol(s) into the glass.*
3. *Pour the non-alcoholic item into the glass, filling it up to the top.*

Another option is to then take the ingredients in the glass and either shake or stir them.

If soda is to be included, it is added last, topping off the glass.

Up

A drink that is served "Up" is chilled with ice, but then served without it.

The cocktail ingredients are typically placed in a shaker during preparation, but are sometimes stirred at the guest's request.

The drink is strained directly into a glass, which ideally is cold.

One example of a cocktail that is usually served this way is the Martini.

Martini glasses can either be maintained cold (by being stored in a refrigerator) or chilled at the time of service by being filled with ice water, which is thrown out before pouring the drink into the glass.

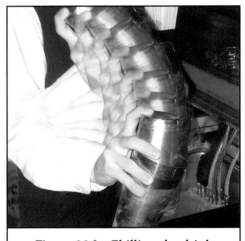

Figure 226: Chilling the drink

Figure 227: Serving "Up"

Neat

A drink requested "Neat" signals to the bartender that the cocktail is served plain. That means it is not chilled with ice or had any other ingredient added.

The alcohol is simply poured into the glass and served to the customer.

A Neat serving can be presented in different kinds of glasses.

The restaurant usually chooses the type of glass that should be used.

Some examples are below (from left to right): a Rock glass, a Taster or Sherry glass, and a Snifter.

Figure 228: Glass options for serving a cocktail "Neat"

Frozen

A cocktail served "Frozen" means that the alcohol(s) is blended with ice.

Drink has a slushy texture and often contains fruit flavors, like the example in Figure 229.

Figure 229: A "Frozen" drink

Figure 230: Add ingredients to the blender

Figure 231: Blend until smooth

The steps to make a frozen drink are:
1. All ingredients for the cocktail, including ice, are placed into a mixer (Figure 230).
2. Blend until the texture is smooth and free of ice chunks, in Figure 231.

Garnish

A number of cocktails add a garnish, which complements the taste of the drink. Some places have the server add the garnish the drinks, while the bartender does it in other locations.

To hold garnishes, many places use a compartmentalized box (Figure 232) that is often called a fruit-bar or condiment-dispenser. It is often placed on the service bar.

The most common garnishes for cocktails are:

- *Olives*
- *Onion*
- *Lime Twist*
- *Lemon Twist*
- *Lime or Lemon Wedge*
- *Celery Stick*
- *Orange Slice*
- *Sherry*
- *Pineapple*
- *Flag (a cherry and an orange slice put together on a stick)*

Figure 232: Fruit Bar example

There are also more unusual garnishes, such as cucumber slices, kiwi, dill or other fruits and vegetables.

Sometimes, the type of garnish can influence the name of a cocktail. For example, a Martini ordered with onions (actually pearl onions) instead of the traditional olives, changes the name to a Martini Gimlet. If the guest orders a Dirty Martini, the preparation dictates that some of the liquid in which the olives are stored should be added to the drink.

The different ways a garnish can be placed in the drink include:
- *Inside the drink.*
- *Sitting on the top of the drink, when the texture allows it.*
- *Split on the rim of the glass.*

4 | Wine Essentials

This section reviews:

- **Wine Categories.**

- **Steps to Making Wine.**

- **Main Categories of Wine.**

- **Common Terms used by Wine Professionals.**

- **Food Pairing.**

SECTION FOUR

Wine Essentials

Objectives

By the end of this section, you should be able to...

- Explain how wine labels differ depending on where they are grown or produced.

- List the four (4) conditions that impact how wine turns out.

- Explain the difference between Champagne and Sparkling wine.

- List the four (4) major categories of wine and give and example of each.

- Explain how wines get their color.

- Descibe the meaning of the 63 most common terms used to describe wine.

Wine Essentials

Organization of Wines

All wines are generally put into one of two categories:
Old World and New World

This does not necessarily refer to the way the wine is made, but the way it is referred to on the label.

In the United States, Chile and Australia, among other countries, wines are referred to by their varietal name. Examples include: Kistler Chardonnay from California, Morandé Cabernet from Chile, and Peter Lehman Shiraz from Australia.

In places like France, Italy and Spain, you'll only find the names of the towns or vineyards on the bottles and that's about it.

<u>Here's why</u>. After centuries of trial and error, winemakers in Europe, mostly France, discovered which grapes grew best in a certain area. **These regions became identified with these grapes.** *So, if you saw a bottle of red wine from Burgundy, you knew it was Pinot Noir.* Certain towns or vineyards desiring to highlight the distinct characteristics - or "terroir" - of their wines only put the name of the town or the vineyards on the label.

The feeling is that it is not the grape that is important so much as where that grape is grown.

Winemakers from the New World are beginning to discover the importance of this type of identification by making it clear on the bottle where a particular wine came from.

However, most winemakers outside of Europe put the grape type (variety) name on the bottle. This makes it much easier on the consumer, who may not know the difference between Gevrey-Chambertin and Hermitage. There are some well-known European exceptions who put the varietal names on the bottle. One example is Alsace, in northeastern France and Germany.

RED, WHITE AND ROSÉ WINES

Red wine does not result from merely squeezing red grapes. All grape juice is nearly the same color--a mostly clear, straw-colored liquid.

The color of red wine comes from the pigmentation (color) in the skin of red grapes. By leaving the grapes skins in with the juice, it takes on the color of the skin. The longer the skins are left with the juice, the more color the juice gets.

It is possible to make a white wine from red grapes. How? The pressed juice is separated from the skins as soon as possible.

In the case of white grapes, winemakers will sometimes leave the fermenting wine in contact with the skins for a period of time to let the flavor and yellow color infuse the juice.

Rosé, pink or blush wines usually come from limited contacted with the skins prior to fermentation, although it is legal in most countries to blend in a little red wine into a white wine to achieve the desired color level.

SPARKLING WINES

Certainly the most festive of all wines are those we call sparkling or bubbly wines. These are often incorrectly called Champagne. **Only the sparkling wine that comes from the Champagne region of France can truly be referred to as Champagne.**

As mentioned before, <u>*the by-product of yeast-sugar reaction is alcohol and carbon dioxide.*</u> When making still wine (wine without bubbles), the gas is released into the atmosphere. *When making sparkling wine, the CO_2 is trapped in the bottle.*

There are a number of ways to keep the gas inside the wine. The most common way (and the one that produces the highest quality product) is the méthode Champenoise. After a still wine is fermented, a yeast and sugar solution known as *"liqueur de tirage"* is put into the wine.

The wine is then placed in a tightly sealed bottle and preferably stored in a cool cellar or cave. **The *liqueur de tirage* causes a second fermentation inside the bottle, trapping the alcohol and carbon dioxide gas.**

After about four weeks, the yeast die and the second fermentation process is complete.

Winemakers may choose to leave the now sparkling wine in contact with the dead yeast cells for a little or a long time. This creates the characteristic sparkling wine flavor known as toast.

After the yeast dies, there is the problem of removing it from the sparkling wine. **The famous Champagne house Veuve Clicquot developed a removal process in the 19th century that has more or less remained unchanged. It is called "riddling".**

Every day the bottles are turned and shaken slightly to loosen any stuck yeast cells. The wine is stored in racks that hold the bottles by the neck. Each day the bottle is tipped a little higher to move the sediment down the bottle and finally in the tip near the cork.

Eventually, the bottles are nearly vertical in the rack, known as a pupitres. *Once the sediment has come to rest near the cork, the neck of the bottle is frozen.* The stopper is removed and the pressure in the bottle pushes out the ice chunk along with the ice-encased sediment.

The bottles are topped off with little sparkling wine from another bottle. Sometimes a small amount of liquid sugar is added to give the wine its desired sweetness. The wine is then corked and labeled.

AROMATIZED WINES

Aromatized wines essentially are still wines that have flavors added to them. *These wines, known as Vermouths,* typically come from areas that produce average quality bulk wines. *Winemakers use herbs, spices, roots and bark to give the wine its desired flavor.* Aromatized wines come in red and white, sweet and dry.

FORTIFIED WINES

Fortified wines are made by adding a neutral grain spirit or brandy to a still wine. *The spirit can be added to the wine before the fermentation process is finished to create sweet wine--as is the case with* **Port.** *Or the spirit can be added after the wine is made to create a dry wine--as is the case with* **Sherry** (although some sherry makers add sugar later to create a sweeter versions). Besides sherry, which historically comes from Jerez, Spain, and Port, there are two other popular fortified wines:

Madeira from the island of Madeira in Portugal, and
Marsala from the island of Sicily in Italy.

Basic Principles of Winemaking

For 1000's of years, people have made wine out of just about any kind of fruit - not just grapes.

The two things required to make wine (otherwise known as vinification) are: sugar and yeast.
For this book, we'll limit the discussion to wine made from grapes.

Four conditions impact the final outcome of the wine:
1. *The grape type;*
2. *Where the vines are grown and the variations in weather conditions;*
3. *What kind of soil the vines grow in;*
4. *And most importantly, the grape grower and winemaker (this is sometimes the same person). Decisions made in the field and in the winery have a great influence on the wine's quality, quantity, flavor, and aroma, among many other characteristics.*

The winemaking process begins once the grapes are harvested. *The wine grower measures the acidity, sugar levels of the grapes,* and the overall level of ripeness of the crop to make the final decision when to harvest. *The grapes can be gathered either manually or by machine.*

They are de-stemmed and repeated crushed to break the skin of the grapes. Pressing releases the juice from grapes. Sometimes yeast is added or the winemaker will rely on natural yeast found on the skin of the grapes to start the fermentation.

When yeast is introduced to sugar-laden juice, the yeast starts consuming the sugar. The by-product of this process is carbon dioxide and alcohol. As the yeast continues to consume the sugars, more CO_2 gas (which dissipates into the air) and alcohol is made. This process will continue until the yeast dies.

The yeast die when:
1. *All the sugars are consumed;*
2. *The alcohol content rises above 15%;*
3. *The temperature of the wine rises above 90 degrees Fahrenheit.*

The level of sweetness can be changed during the fermentation process by either stopping it or adding unfermented grape juice to the mix. Wines can be aged in barrels or stainless steel tanks after the desired level of fermenting is complete. Generally, wines are filtered for clarity.

The Main Grapes

There are five different species of grape-bearing vines and hundreds of varieties of wine growing grapes.

We will only address several of the most popular grapes used for wine production.

WHITES

Chardonnay

The most well-known grape in the world, Chardonnay can be found in nearly every winegrowing region in the world. Its origins are hard to pin down, but like so many grape varieties it was first mastered in France.

The most elegant and expensive Chardonnay comes from France's Burgundy region. **White Burgundy (all white wines from Burgundy are 100% Chardonnay) has also become most copied style of Chardonnay.** However, few winemakers outside of Burgundy have matched the buttery, spicy, lemony qualities found in the wines made in the towns of Meursault, Puligny-Montrachet and Chassagne-Montrachet.

The Burgundy style copied the world over is due to its use of oak barrels. The wine could use oak either during the fermentation process and/or while aging.

Another style of Chardonnay somes from the Chablis area, which is northwest of the main Burgundy region. Here the wines are anything <u>but</u> buttery. They are fermented in stainless steel tanks and may or may not see any oak barrels during the aging process.

Chablis wines are best described as flinty and mineral-like with a crisp, clean acidity. A few growing regions, including New Zealand, have chosen to copy this style of Chardonnay.

Figure 233: White Grapes

Reisling

One of the most desirable wines of the world. *Often associated with the vineyards of Germany, especially those along the Rhine and Mosel Rivers, Riesling is grown in many places throughout the world.* The grape enjoys a cooler climate and can be found in France's Alsace region, Australia, New York State, California and Washington State, where it is often called Johannisberg Riesling.

The image many people have of Riesling is that is always sweet and somewhat less desirable.

Being one of the most adaptable wine-making grapes, Riesling comes in every category from the very dry (no residual sugar) to very sweet (high percentage of residual sugar).

Sauvignon Blanc

Typically found in cooler wine growing areas, Sauvignon Blanc wine comes in more or less two styles. **There is the hay-like grass version.** These wines have the smell of fresh-cut grass and green plums.

The other is the melon style. You'll find this style of Sauvignon Blanc in the warmer climates and it will be a little more robust than the more acidic, refreshing grassy style. The melon style offers tastes of melons and

apricots. **Often, this type of wine will spend a little or a lot of time in oak barrels, which gives it a creamy, vanilla aroma and taste.**

Sauvignon Blanc is grown the world over. *Some of the better regions producing this wine are Bordeaux and the Loire Valley in France, northeastern Italy, New Zealand, South Africa, Chile, Washington State and California.*

Pinot Gris

Growing in popularity, **Pinot Gris is often at its best when it is made in a light, crisp, acidic style.**

Pinot Gris has a mineral and lemon flavors and is an excellent companion to light fish dishes. It is especially enjoyable during hotter weather when it can be quite refreshing.

Pinot Gris from France's Alsace region can be a bit more robust in flavor than most other Pinot Gris. In Alsace it is called Tokay d'Alsace Pinot Gris.

In addition to Alsace, you can find Pinot Gris in northeastern Italy, where it is called Pinot Grigio, Oregon and California.

REDS

Cabernet Sauvignon

One of the most royal and one of the most common wines are the ones made with Cabernet Sauvignon. It can be blended in some of the finest and most expensive Bordeaux or used all by itself, such as those made in Napa Valley, California. It is also made in garden variety styles in just about every growing region in the world and comes in a wide range of prices.

The Cabernet Sauvignon grape is very small and has a thick skin. This translates into a high skin-to-juice ratio, which makes the wine taste very astringent or harsh. In addition, Cabernet Sauvignon has naturally high acidity. In the right hands, a deep, dark powerful wine can be made out of these grapes. In the hands of the less adept, the wines can be overwhelming and difficult to palate.

Many winemakers follow the lead of Bordeaux wineries and blend Cabernet Sauvignon with mellower wines, such as Merlot, to take off its rough edges. Australian winemakers have had particular success with blending Cabernet Sauvignon with Shiraz.

In addition to Bordeaux and Australia, excellent Cabernet Sauvignon and Cabernet Sauvignon-based wines can be found in Italy, Spain, Chile, California and Long Island, NY.

Merlot

Often very fruity with blackberry jam-like qualities, Merlot has grown in popularity in recent years, especially with those exploring red wine for the first time. It is a wine that is very easy to like since it is mellow, fruity and often not very complicated.

The classic home of Merlot is Bordeaux on the east bank of the Dordogne River in France.

Winemakers blend Merlot with Cabernet Sauvignon and other red varieties to give the simple Merlot-based wine more structure. In the United States, winemakers produce wines made of 100% Merlot, however many winemakers take a cue from Bordeaux and add a little Cabernet Sauvignon to give these jam-like, fruity wines a little more intensity and interesting flavors.

Winemakers in Chile, Italy, California and Washington State are capitalizing on Merlot's growing popularity.

Pinot Noir

One of the most difficult grapes to grow and to make into wine, Pinot Noir is one of the most popular and most food friendly wines in the world. Most wine lovers associate Pinot Noir with red wine from Burgundy, where they make wine from 100% Pinot Noir grapes. *Several of the highly prized vineyards in Burgundy produce some of the most expensive wines in the world.*

Other areas around the globe have had great success with Pinot Noir, especially winemakers in Oregon. *Despite being a red grape, Pinot Noir is one of the primary grapes used to make Champagne.*

Syrah / Shiraz

Syrah is one of the main grapes found in the steep river valleys of France's northern Rhône. **It is a full-bodied, spicy wine that also provides the drinker with delicious blackberry, black currant and plum characteristics. In the middle of the 19th century, Syrah was introduced to Australia, where it is known as Shiraz.** Since then, it has become one of the most widely planted grapes in the country. Australian winemakers produce a variety of styles from low-quality jug wines to wines of great international renown, such as the famous Grange Hermitage. They have also had great success blending Shiraz with varieties such as Cabernet Sauvignon, Merlot and Grenache. *You can also find Syrah (or Sirah as it is sometimes spelled) in California and Italy.*

Zinfandel

Once thought to be related to the Primitivo grape of southern Italy, researchers have traced the origins of the Zinfandel grape back to Croatia's Crljenak grape.

Regardless of its scientific geneology, **American vintners claim Zinfandel as the only "true" winemaking grape in North America.** *Historically known for making big, fruity, zesty wines that are often high in alcohol, most people now associate Zinfandel with the blush (or rosé) version known as white Zinfandel.* In addition to the hotter California wine growing regions, winemakers cultivate this grape in Brazil and South Africa.

Figure 234: Red Grapes

Common Terms

Acidic
A term to describe a wine tartness. It can indicate unfavorable characteristics when there is excess acid in the wine.

Appearance
The way a wine looks, which can range from "crystalline" to "cloudy". Some wines appear dark as ink while others watery. A cloudy appearance may indicate a wine is unfiltered or perhaps has problems due to age or improper storage.

Amarone
Italian for "strongly bitter". This is a process of winemaking classically found in the Veneto region of Italy. The grape bunches are harvested and left on racks for several months. This allows the moisture in the grapes to evaporate leaving behind a nectar that is high in sugar. These grapes are then pressed and fermented. If the process is stopped before the wine is completely fermented, the wine is known as recioto. If fermentation is allowed to convert all the sugar to alcohol, the wine becomes an amorone. Amarone wines are known for their
relatively high alcohol content.

Appassimento
Appassire in Italian means "to dry" or "to wither". Thus, appassimento is the process of making wine in the Valpolicella, Italy, from partially raisinated grapes, a holdover from the days when man first learned to preserve fruit by drying it.

Approved viticultural area (AVA)
A growing region defined by the Bureau of Alcohol, Tobacco and Firearms, the federal agency that governs the production of wine in the United States.

Appellation Contrôlée
French wine law that spells out specific growing regions, wine label information and growing, harvesting and fermentation criteria.

Appellation d'origine Contrôlée
The highest category of quality wines under French wine law. AOC producers must follow strict guidelines for growing, harvesting and fermenting grapes and the subsequent labeling. Among other rules, AOC rules specify vineyards, districts, towns and regions where certain grapes can be grown.

Balance
When all the taste components - acids, tannins, fruit, among others - work harmoniously together, the wine is considered in balance. When one of these components overpowers the others, the wine is considered out of balance.

Barrel aging
After wines are fermented, they are often placed in oak barrels to receive the tastes from the wood and to soften some of the harsh characteristics of young wines.

Barrel fermentation
The process of fermenting wines in small casks, usually made of oak, instead of large stainless steel or wooden tanks. While more expensive and less controllable than steel tanks, the procedure gives the wine a creaminess and subtle oak flair. Barrel fermentation is usually reserved for white wines, such as Chardonnay and Sauvignon Blanc.

Big
A term used to describe full-bodied, rich wines.

Blanc de noirs
Literally "white of black" in French, this term indicates a white or blush wine made from red grapes. It is typically reserved for sparkling wines made from the Pinot Noir and Pinot Meunier. It is occasionally used for still blush wines made from red grapes.

Blanc de blancs
Literally "white of white" in French, this term indicates a white wine made entirely from white grapes. It is typically only said for sparkling wines made from 100% Chardonnay grapes. Blanc de blanc wines are usually light and delicate.

Body
The perceived weight of wine, which is actually a combination of alcohol, extract, glycerol and acid. A full-bodied wine displays rich, complex, powerful characteristics. A light-bodied wines are generally more simple and lack the powerful tastes of a full-bodied wine. Medium-bodied wines are in the middle. Light-bodied wine does not mean low quality. A great light- or medium-body wine may offer finesse and other refined characteristics.

Bordeaux, Bordeaux-style wines

A red wine (unless otherwise indicated as a white Bordeaux or a sweet Bordeaux) that is a blend of two or more of the following grape varietals: Cabernet Sauvignon, Merlot, Cabernet Franc, Petit Verdot and Malbec. To a lesser extent, winemakers may also use Gross Verdot, Carmenere and St. Macaire. A white Bordeaux blend could include Sauvignon Blanc, Mucadelle and Sémillon.

Bouquet

Often confused with aroma, bouquet refers to the complex fragrances that develop as a wine ages in a bottle.

Botrytis cinerea

Also known as noble rot, pourriture nobile (France), Edelfäule (Germany) and Muffa nobile (Italy), *this mold attacks grapes draining them of moisture but leaving behind a highly concentrated nectar found in many dessert wines.* This disease occurs only in certain environmental conditions.

Breathing

Exposing the wine to air prior to drinking. While some disagree, people who believe in letting wine "breath" or "aerate" say it softens the tannins in younger red wines and allows complex bouquets to develop in older wines. Generally, lower quality reds, white wine and very old wine do not benefit and may diminish from their exposure to air.

Burgundy

A winemaking region south of Dijon France known for making some of the world's best Pinot Noir and Chardonnay wines. Winemakers in the United States have used the term generically to mean red wine.

Brut

A term applied to the driest of sparkling wines. That is they contain very little residual sugar. Extra brut indicates a wine that is extremely or totally dry.

Cava
Spanish term for sparkling wine. These wine typically come from Spain's northern winemaking regions and must be made using the méthode champenoise.

Chablis
The northernmost region of Burgundy, France, known for outstanding Chardonnay wines. Winemakers in the United States have used the term generically to mean a white wine.

Champagne
A region in France known for its sparkling wines. Winemakers in the United States have used the term generically to mean sparkling wine.

Corked
A descriptor that indicates the wine has been tainted by a chemical compound called 246 tricloroanisol or 246-TCA. This chemical is found in some corks and can be detected by humans at extremely low levels, as little as 30 parts per trillion. The chemical gives wine a musty taste of wet cardboard or damp newspapers.

Decanting
Decanting either separates wine from particulates and sediment deposited during the aging process or to soften assertive young wines. It can also be done with most any wine to show the server's skill and add flair to a guest's dining experience.

Dry
A wine without any residual sugar is considered dry. During the fermentation process, yeast turns sugars found in the grape juice into alcohol and carbon dioxide gas.

If these sugars are completely consumed, the wine is considered dry. If a noticeable amount of sugar is left in the wine, it is considered off-dry.

Earthy
A wine tasting term used to describe tastes or aromas usually associated with damp soil.

Edelfäule
See botrytis cinerea.

Enophile
Lover of wine.

Finish
The final impression left from a taste of wine. A lingering, distinctive "finish" speaks well for a wine. A short or lacking finish signals a lower quality wine.

Grand cru
The French phrase for "great growth" has slightly different meanings throughout France. In essence, *grand cru indicates grapes were grown in ideal or special locals,* which could be an area of a vineyard, a district containing several vineyards, or a designation given to a particular wine producer.

Green
Most often, green refers to a wine that is too young to drink. However, green can be used to describe wine made from under-ripe grapes. These wines often are quite high in acid but lack in fruit flavor.

Hot
A wine tasting term used to describe wines high in alcohol.
Overly hot wines give a burning sensation in the throat and mouth and are considered *out of balance.*

Legs
The wine "tears" found on the inside of a glass after swirling the wine. The presence of legs usually indicates a wine is rich and full-bodied.

Meritage
A Bordeaux-style wine that is usually red. See Bordeaux.

Méthode Champenoise
A process of making sparkling wine in which a finished still wine has yeast and sugar added to it and is then rebottled. This "dosage", as it is called, creates a second fermentation in the wine. As with any fermentation, the sugars are converted to alcohol and carbon dioxide by the yeast. Since the fermentation takes place in a closed bottle, the CO_2 gas is absorbed into the wine. It is this absorbed gas that gives sparkling wines their bubbles or sparkle. Once the second fermentation is complete, the dead yeast cells are removed through a process of riddling (regularly turning the bottles as they sit topside down in racks so the sediment settles at the opening of the bottle) and disgorging (chilling the bottles to reduce the pressure in the bottle, thus allowing the sediment to be gently pushed out). The final pressure in a standard bottle of sparkling wine can range from 60 to 90 pounds per square inch. Caution should always be used when opening sparkling wines.

Muffa nobile
See Botrytis Cinerea.

Musky
Term used to describe a wine that presents earthy characteristics.

Noble Rot
See botrytis cinerea.

Oxidized
Term generally used to describe a wine that has decayed due to either poor storage (often overheated) or exposed to air by accident. Often noticeable at sight by a change of the color of the wine to a light brown color, the taste veers to a light nutty and sherry like flavor.

Oxygenation
See "Breathing"

Off-dry
See "Dry".

Passed
A wine that has passed its maturity level and is starting to degrade.

Port, Porto
A sweet fortified wine typically served after the meal. Port comes in several varieties including vintage, ruby and tawny. Tawny ports are lighter in color and have a brown sugar and raisin taste. The other ports are deep red to brown with a fruitier taste. Vintage ports, which can age 50 years or more, have a good deal of sediment and must be decanted. Porto indicates the wine is shipped from the city of Oporto, Portugal, the classic home of this wine.

Punt
Indentation in the bottom of a wine or sparkling wine bottle. The punt give the bottle more structural integrity and also serves to catch sediment.

Rhône
An arrid wine growing region along the Rhône river in southern France known for Syrahs, Viognier and many other grapes.

Ripasso
The addition of juice from select Valpolicella grapes to the pomace leftover from the fermentation of Amarone. When the young wine from the previous year's harvest is added to the rich, wine-soaked skins, a second process of fermentation is encouraged which imparts color, tannin, fruit and alcohol to the mix. The resulting wine still possesses some of the fresh character of classic Valpolicella, but also exhibits additional complexity and richness very similar to Amarone.

Pomace
Leftover from the grapes after they were pressed to extract the juice. This residue can potentially be used further to make brandy.

Sekt
Term used for sparkling wine in Germany and other German-speaking areas. True German sekt is usually fruity and little sweeter than its counterparts in France, Spain, Italy and the United States.

Smoky
Tasting term used to describe the smoke-like qualities in a wine's aroma and taste. It is something akin to a light campfire or flint smoke.

Soft
A term used to describe a wine that is mellow and without the harshness normally associated with tannin and acid. Soft implies good balance.

Sur lie
French for "on the lees". Lees is the sediment left over after fermentation. It can contain dead yeast cells, grape skins, grape pits, particles of vine and grape leaves.

Winemakers leave their wine sur lie to increase complexity and improve flavor in a wine. Sparkling wines made in the méthode champenoise necessarily are left on the lees because yeast is added to the wine after it has been put into the bottle. Wines that that have been made sur lie generally gain a creamy, yeasty, fresh bread quality.

Terroir
A French word meaning the entire environment encompassing the vineyard, including the soil, subsoil, weather conditions and its position in relation to the Sun.

Texture
An impression of weight that a wine gives when it is on the palate (or mouth). It derives from a wine's glycerin among other factors, which make the wine seem thicker than water. Wines lacking or absent of texture are referred to as thin or watery.

Toasty
A term used to describe toasted bread characteristics in a wine's aroma or taste. Toasty characteristics are often found in sparkling wines and in some Chardonnays.

Trocken
German for "dry".

Ullage
Air space created in the top of barrels and bottles due to evaporation. Ullage in older wines may be a product of the natural aging process. Ullage in younger wines generally indicates a problem with the cork.

Unbalanced
When one or more of a wine's taste components-acids, tannins, fruit, among others-dominates over the others, the wine is considered unbalanced.

Unctuous
A descriptor used for a wine that is extremely sweet, rich and has a heavy, almost oily texture.

Vanilla
A descriptor used for wines with a vanilla-like aroma or taste. Vanilla qualities usually come from time spent by a wine in an oak barrel during and/or after fermentation. Some winemakers also use oak chips and extracts to achieve the tastes and smells of vanilla.

Vin de pays
French for "wine of the country". It is the third lowest quality level for French wines, just above the lowest quality level, vin de table. Producers of vin de pays enjoy fewer restrictions and are allowed higher grape yields than the two highest quality levels, vin délimité de qualité supérieure and appellation d'origine contrôlée, which is the highest level of quality. Vin de pays should not be confused with vin du pays, which means local wine and has no legal meaning.

Vitis vinifera
A species of grapevine that is most commonly associated with winemaking. It is native to Europe as well as East and Central Asia, but has been planted worldwide.

Yeasty
A descriptor used for wines that have spent time sur lie, which means on the dead yeast and grape sediment after fermentation is finished. Yeasty can be best described as having tastes and aromas of fresh bread or bread dough. While desirable in sparkling wines and certain white wines, it is considered a flaw in most wines.

Food and Wine Pairing

Much has been written about food and wine pairing. For practical purposes here, the best guide would be to keep it simple. There is no definitive theory on matching wine to food, but a couple of simple concepts should allow you to make competent selections when a guest, chef or event planner calls you on to pick a wine.

POWER WITH POWER

The first rule of thumb is to match power with power. *What we mean when we say match power with power is that wine, like food, has a certain power level or intensity?* Think about a nice, crisp Sauvignon Blanc from the Sancerre region in France. This is a light, fresh, fruity wine. It's fair to say that this is not a powerful wine.

Now, think of a thick Moroccan lamb stew with garlic mashed potatoes and grilled vegetables. Is "light" the first word that comes to mind when you think of this dish? No, this is a heavy, meaty dish. Not only is the meat rich and fatty, the preparation has lots of spices and the sauce is thick and heavy. This dish ranks high on the power scale. So, the Sancerre is probably not a good choice based on the power with power guideline.

Competent food wine pairing also means knowing which wines not to recommend. The lamb dish would overwhelm even the most powerful white wine. This eliminates all whites and indeed many lighter reds, such as Beaujolais, most Pinot Noirs, most Chiantis and many Rioja wines. This dish calls for something along the lines of a Cabernet Sauvignon, Syrah or spicy red Zinfandel to match the intensity of flavors in the lamb dish.

COMPLEMENT OR CONTRAST

Once you understand the power with power rule, there are really **no wrong choices from this point on, just matters of opinion.** The next step in food and wine pairing is deciding whether to complement or contrast the flavors in the dish.

<u>*Let's use another example.*</u> Your guest orders a grilled salmon with a lemon-dill butter sauce. Salmon is pretty fatty and rich. The same can be said for the sauce. You can go one of two ways here. It really depends upon the situation and what you want to do.

Do you want to emphasize the richness of this dish?

In other words, do you want to mimic the charcoal flavors of this fish and the butteriness of the sauce? If you said yes, then you would be advocating a complementary wine. Let's choose a big, creamy Chardonnay, like the ones often made in California, Australia and Chile. These would be decadent, indulgent choices of wine. And that's OK provided the situation calls for it.

Why do we use terms like indulgent and luxurious to describe this suggestion? It might be best to think about the interaction of flavors going on in one's mouth. You take bite of the fish after swirling it around in the sauce. You taste the butter in the sauce and the fatty fish flavors and then there's that yummy charcoal spiciness left over. You take a sip of wine. Lo and behold, you taste nearly the same things. There's the creaminess that comes from the time the wine spent in oak barrels. After you swallow you're left with the unmistakable taste of cloves and nutmeg spices. Each bite and sip builds on the previous bite and sip.

Figure 235: Explore different food / wine pairings

When would this type of complementing suggestion be appropriate? That's hard to say. It may come down to personalities of those drinking it. You may want to think of the reason for the meal. Is it a birthday, anniversary or some other kind of celebration? This would be a time for less restraint in the meal. The wine pairing should reflect that indulgent attitude.

Now, Let's consider Contrasting

Take the same dish, but pair it with a Chablis, an unoaked Chardonnay from New Zealand or a crisp, lemony Muscadet from the Loire Valley, France. The highlight of these wines is their acid, which tastes like the refreshing sensation you find in a green apple or some tropical fruits.

Let's again take a bite of salmon, but we then take sip of the Chablis, which lacks the creaminess and spiciness of the first wine. The crispness of the wine and the bracing acidity cleanses your mouth of the heavy, buttery, creamy sensations coating the inside of your mouth. It puts you back to where you were before you took a bite.

Personal preferences should again dictate on whether the contrasting wine is suggested. But also consider the situation. Perhaps this is a business lunch or maybe the guests are dining outside in the early summer. Can you see how you might show some restraint with the choice of wine?

ADVANCED PAIRING

Can food and wine pairing be more complicated? *Obviously it can.* There are many great books written on this subject, in fact. There may be specific flavors in the food that can be highlighted with certain wines.

You may also want to emphasize regional characteristics of the food and wine, choucroute with a crisp, fruity Alsatian Riesling for example.

At this level of pairing, however, you must become more familiar with the unique tastes of wine varietals and how winemakers, vintages and regions influence them. You must also become aware of the different food tastes and preparations. These and other factors can play important role in the selection of the wine, but expertise in food and wine pairing comes with time and experience.

Advanced Wine Service

Wine essentials of opening a standing wine bottle as well as the service steps for white, red and sparkling wine can be found in The Professional Service Guide

Vol 3: Service Essentials. Here we cover the advanced techinque of opening cradled wine and the art of decanting.

OPENING IN A BASKET

To open a bottle of wine presented in a basket requires the same utensils as a vertical bottle. They are a B&B plate, a wine key and a napkin, as in Figure 236. Some professionals' use an extra B&B plate, depending on how low the neck of the bottle rests in the basket.

Figure 236: Utensiles for opening

The main reason for presenting a wine in a basket is usually to maintain the bottle in the same position in which it was stored.

This avoids agitating the wine, which can cause sediment to mix with the wine. Basket presentation is justified by older red wines, which may need decanting (a service to remove sediment.) However, there are times in which a wine is presented in a basket just for show, and not decanted.

The first thing to observe after having set the bottle in the basket is whether or not the wine reaches the cork. If it does not, then proceed with opening the bottle.

If the wine is in contact with the cork, place a B&B plate up side down under the front of the basket (Figure 236). This raises the bottle's neck until the wine flows back into the bottle, preventing wine spillage during opening.

Another rule to respect is that if a bottle is introduced to the table in a horizontal position, it should never reach a vertical position. Do not defeat the purpose for which it was left laying down.

Remove the foil completely from the bottle. Clean the top / neck of the bottle to ensure no contaminents get into the wine while its being poured.

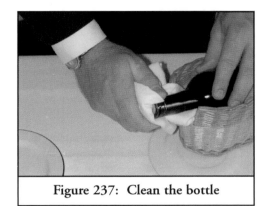

Figure 237: Clean the bottle

Next, twist your wine opener into the center of the cork.

Maintain a vertical line between the spiral and the bottle. Do not push-in, but twist-in.

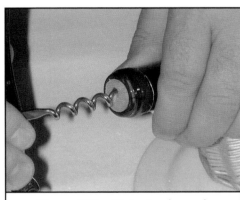

Figure 238: Twist in the cork

Twist the spiral deep through the cork in a way that you will still be able to lock the corkscrew lever against the rim of the bottleneck.

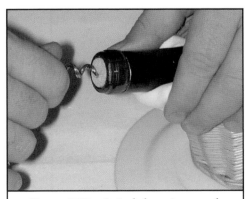

Figure 239: Spiral deep into cork

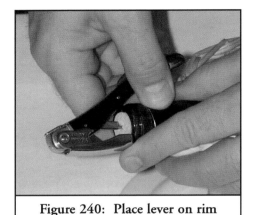

Figure 240: Place lever on rim

Once you are comfortable that the twist is sufficiently deep within the cork, maintain the lever of the corkscrew against the rim by the use of a finger from the holding hand.

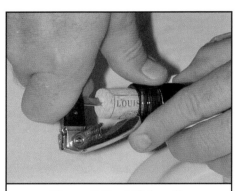

Figure 241: Lift handle

Then pull out the cork by lifting the handle, as demonstrated in Figure 241. This procedure is easier if you push off the rim of the bottleneck with your thumb.

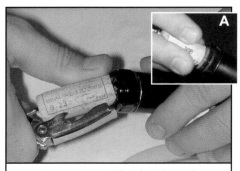

Figure 242: Slowly tilt cork

When the cork is almost out, slowly tilt the cork before completing the extraction. This allows air into the bottle and breaks the vacuum created by pulling on the cork. Another way to proceed with the final removal of the cork is to grab the ensemble of the cork and the lever, then extract everthing with the help of all four fingers and the thumb, seen in Figure 242, 'A'.

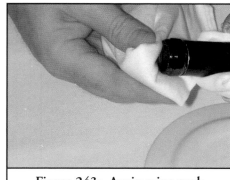

Figure 243: Again wipe neck

It is a good idea to again wipe the neck of the bottle. Cork and foil should be presented to the guest.

Figure 244: Pick up glass to pour

A taste is poured for the host to accept the wine. When pouring, keep the bottle's movement to a minimum. Pick up the glass from the table and tilt it, as seen in Figure 244.

Figure 245: Display bottle

As the guest tastes the wine, present the wine by the left side, as in Figure 245.

——————— DECANTING WINE ———————

There are two technical reasons for decanting wine: to remove sediment, and for aeration. There is also an element of show in decanting. Show is and must remain completely subjective, and should not be influenced solely by the purchase price of the bottle.

To remove the sediments

Any red wine that is approximate ten (10) years old may contain sediment, regardless of the grape, and should be decanted. There is no difference between grapes that reduces the risk of developing sediment. Whether Pinot Noir, Burgundy, or Bordeaux, if a bottle is a decade old, it needs to be decanted.

To aerate the wine

Aeration exposes the wine to the air in order to help that wine achieve an improved taste. Aeration is not only for older wines. Decanting younger wines improves the taste before drinking. As more and more wines are consumed before reaching maturity, decanting for the purpose of aeration is becoming more popular.

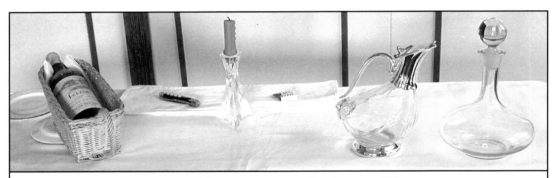

Figure 246: Equipment used to Decant Wine

The action of decanting is extremely simple. It is more difficult to open a bottle of wine properly than it is to decant it. Decanting can be performed on a guéridon, a side stand, a specific table reserved for this use, or even a small table that remains by the guest's table. It can also be done on a bus tray covered with a napkin, set by the guest's table on a tray stand.

The two main styles of carafes are displayed above in Figure 246: With a spout (left) and without (right). The decanter on the right can also be referred to as a Nautical Decanter, for it was often used in sailing vessels to place wine on the table. Bottles would have tipped over due to the rocking of the boat.

The following utensils are needed (in Figure 246) to decant:

- A decanting carafe
- A candle holder with a candle (preferably dripless)
- A wine cradle
- A good wine key
- Two napkins
  ○ One to save the tablecloth from potential drips made by mistake.
  ○ One to wipe the neck of the bottle.
- Two B&B plates
- A book of matches or a lighter

Opening

Whether the bottle is presented to the table in a wine cradle (Figure 247) or upright depends on how the wine was stored.

If the bottle was stored horizontally (done in order to keep the cork from drying out and consequently letting air into the bottle) and there is a risk for sediment, it will have formed on the bottom side of the bottle.

The bottle should then never reach the vertical position, in order to avoid having the sediment fall into the wine. Bottles are occasionally handled vertically, however, when guests are allowed to bring their own wine to the establishment.

It is best to set the bottle vertically a few

days before opening it. This allows the sediment to settle to the bottom of the bottle. This is not always possible when guests bring their own bottle.

When opening a bottle that is to be decanted, the entire foil should be removed. This allows the best possible cleaning of the bottle's neck, thus assuring that wine will not be contaminated should it drip along the neck of the bottle before going into the carafe. Since there is no foil on the bottle's neck, the risk of wine tasting metallic from contact with the foil (often made of pewter or lead) is eliminated. Removing the foil also allows the wine to be clearly viewed through the bottle's neck and shoulder, to see the sediment as it approaches.

Figure 247: Clean after removing foil

Figure 248: Remove cork carefully

Figure 249: Provide a taste before decating

When the bottle is opened horizontally, the cork should be tilted slowly before complete extraction, as in Figure 248. This allows air into the bottle and eliminates the vacuum that pulling on the cork creates, thus letting the wine settle back into the bottle. It should be noted that some cradle types have such a low headrest that they require a B&B plate to be placed underneath the cradle to avoid spilling wine after opening.

After opening the bottle by removing the cork, it is a good idea to again wipe the neck of the bottle, for old corks can leave residue.

A taste should be poured to the host for acceptance of the wine before decanting. To do so, and keep the movement of the bottle to a minimum, it is recommended to pick up the tasting glass from the table and to tilt it for pouring. However, there are two exceptions to this rule:

1. A vertically stored bottle: Do not pour a taste, but instead, decant directly without interrupting the pour. Otherwise, the action of switching the bottle back to a vertical position will spread the sediments in the bottle.

2. A horizontally stored bottle without a basket: Avoid pouring a taste, thereby minimizing the movement of liquid in the bottle and upsetting the sediment. Instead, decant directly without interrupting the pour.

Two things that drastically impact the comfort level of a server during decanting *are the position of the candle and the elbow/arm position.*

Depending on the height of the server, the candle should be adjusted in such a way that the body position remains straight while the bottle is in a direct line between the eyes and the candle WITHOUT being above the flame (so as not to heat the wine,) seen in Figure 250. Elbows and arms should be away from the server's side, allowing the bottle to be adjusted to the best viewing position for seeing the light through the wine. A common mistake is to lock the elbows to the sides, which forces the server to adopt awkward positions when adjusting the bottle to see through it.

TIP: When starting to pour, disregard the candle and focus on assuring a safe and stable pour. Only after a smooth pour is achieved, does the server focus on seeing through the bottle.

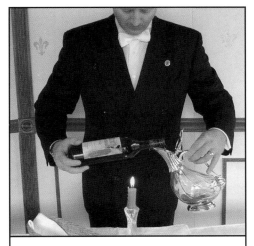

Figure 250: Comfort depends on the candle and elbow position

Pouring

The two styles of pouring correspond to the two different carafe types.

When decanting into a carafe with a spout (Figure 251), do not let the bottle of wine touch the carafe. The spout is designed to catch any drips that run along the neck of the bottle, so there is no need to lean the bottle on the carafe.

Figure 251: Pouring into a spouted carafe

Figure 252: Pouring into a non-spouted carafe

When using a carafe without a spout, it is a requirement to lean the neck of the bottle against the neck of the carafe.

This practice ensures a safe pour.

The decanting technique is extremely simple. Use the light of a candle to watch the movement of potential sediments towards the bottle's neck (Figure 253), and stop pouring before sediment falls into the carafe. When decanting for the purpose of aeration, the use of a candle is not required, unless it is for show.

The smoothness of the wine pour is as important as the handling of the bottle prior to opening. If the pour is too irregular, it will create waves inside the bottle that will mix the sediment with the wine. Keeping the pour smooth is essential to reducing floating sediment.

Figure 253: Use light to see flow

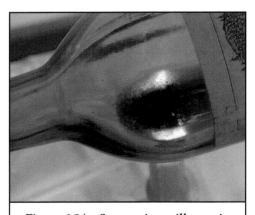

Figure 254: Some wine will remain